PENGUIN BOOKS
THE ASSASSINATION OF RAJIV GANDHI

A journalist for thirty-eight years, Neena Gopal began her career in a Bangalore that was the hotbed of post-Emergency politics. Moving to the UAE in the 1980s, she worked for the Dubai-based *Gulf News* where, as foreign editor, she travelled in the Middle East during and after the first Gulf War in 1990, and Operation Desert Storm, covering war-torn Iraq and its neighbours through the Second Gulf War in 2003. Gopal's other news-hunting ground has been India and its immediate neighbourhood, both as a foreign affairs journalist and as a close observer of the life and times of many leaders in India, Pakistan, Sri Lanka and Afghanistan. She currently edits the Bangalore edition of *Deccan Chronicle*.

The Assassination
of
RAJIV GANDHI

NEENA GOPAL

PENGUIN BOOKS

An imprint of Penguin Random House

PENGUIN BOOKS

USA | Canada | UK | Ireland | Australia
New Zealand | India | South Africa | China | Singapore

Penguin Books is part of the Penguin Random House group of companies
whose addresses can be found at global.penguinrandomhouse.com

Published by Penguin Random House India Pvt. Ltd
4th Floor, Capital Tower 1, MG Road,
Gurugram 122 002, Haryana, India

First published in Viking by Penguin Random House India 2016
Published in Penguin Books 2017

10 9 8 7 6 5 4 3 2

The views and opinions expressed in this book are the author's own and the
facts are as reported by him, which have been verified to the extent possible,
and the publishers are not in any way liable for the same.

ISBN 9780143428985

Typeset in Minion Pro by Manipal Digital Systems, Manipal
Printed at Repro India Limited

www.penguin.co.in

This is a legitimate digitally printed version of the book and therefore might not
have certain extra finishing on the cover.

Contents

Contents

1

The Assassination

RARELY DOES ONE GET A ringside view of a cataclysmic event that changes the course of history in one's own country, let alone a neighbouring one—an event which goes on to alter one's life in a hundred different ways. With Rajiv Gandhi's assassination, nothing was the same again. Everything changed . . .

He must have died instantly, falling face down as the bomb detonated, lying there in a mangled, bloodied heap, only his white-and-red scarf and his outsized running shoes intact. His clothes had been blown off his back; only the top of his head was visible.

In a matter of seconds, a fairly standard report about a charismatic politician on the comeback trail, albeit a Gandhi scion, a former prime minister and barely forty-six at the time, was transformed—tragically—into one of the biggest stories I had ever covered.

It catapulted me from an unknown reporter to someone who would always be known as the last journalist to have interviewed Rajiv Gandhi, minutes before he died. A macabre twist. And not the kind of exclusive I had bargained for.

In the last twenty-five years, every time that night has come up in casual conversation, it has unfailingly recalled the image of Rajiv Gandhi lying on the ground, one outstretched arm sporting the only ostentatious thing about him, the Gucci watch he had been wearing during our hour-long interaction. And yes, his Lotto shoes. As trite as it may sound, it seemed almost as if he had been walking on air that night, exuding confidence that he was on his way back to the prime minister's office.

But there he now lay, cut down in his prime, less than a few feet away from where I stood rooted to the spot, in shock.

I can still recall, in that split second before the explosion, the strange whooshing sound; a series of sputters, followed by a massive, resounding blast accompanied by a great, blinding flash of light. The heat, searing, singeing, knocked me back with its strength, raining death on everyone in front of me.

I didn't know what exactly had happened. I looked around peering through the smoke. There seemed to be no one else in front. Could I really be the last man standing?

Rajiv Gandhi had landed at the Guindy airport, a stone's throw from the more well-known facility at Meenambakam, just before sundown that day, piloting his own plane. A clutch of Congress party workers and some journalists from the local newspapers were there, as were bored policemen who didn't bat an eyelid when I walked into the rooms at one end of the arrival lounge at the airport, which had been earmarked for VVIP guests. I checked out the dank interiors, noted paint peeling from the walls, the terrible toilets, the beds with less than clean sheets, and the complete lack of security. This was where the Congress chief was to be billeted that night.

As Rajiv Gandhi walked into the arrival hall, a long, narrow room, he instantly spotted me and waved me to his side. I couldn't tell whether the hundreds of messages I had bombarded every Congress office with, as Rajiv Gandhi criss-crossed the country on the first leg of the campaign, had been conveyed to him. Either way, after endless telephone calls, I had finally tracked down Rajiv Gandhi's campaign manager and former diplomat, Mani Shankar Aiyar, who had told me on the night of 20 May to be present at Guindy the next day, and promised he would ensure an exclusive interview during the course of Rajiv Gandhi's election halt at Madras (now Chennai). So there I was.

We had met only months before when Rajiv Gandhi, accompanied by his wife, Sonia, had stopped over in Dubai en route to Bombay from Moscow and Tehran. At a reception hosted at the Hyatt Regency by the local Indian community, I had spent time with him discussing the hot topic of the day—his journey by train from Delhi to Lucknow, just after his Z security had been withdrawn. It was only the second time that I met him but he was chatty and approachable, and spoke at length about the drift in India under the new government and the need to rebuild ties with Moscow and Tehran.

Sonia Gandhi, unlike the self-assured, confident leader of the party she is today, was nervous, fidgety and completely out of her comfort zone, asking me repeatedly whether I was recording the conversation with her. Which I was not.

Rajiv Gandhi's pressure on the Chandrashekhar government had ensured that the United States was denied permission to refuel its fighter aircraft in India at the height of the Gulf War. He had been at the receiving end of critical press in the western media for that decision, as it forced the US to continue to refuel from the Indian Ocean island of Diego Garcia. Rajiv Gandhi's Congress party would subsequently pull the plug on the minority Chandrashekhar government, setting in motion the May 1991 polls that would claim his life.

Once I got the heads-up from Aiyar, I scrapped plans to cover Jayalalitha's campaign in her constituency. In fact, on 20 May, while I was standing outside Jayalalitha's tony Poes Garden home in Madras along with a crowd of her die-hard supporters, she had slowed down and stopped her car when she saw me waving and, in response to a request, agreed to let me accompany her the next day when she planned to head to Bodinayakanur, the constituency from where she was standing for elections. She asked me to be there at the crack of dawn.

This was to be the All India Anna Dravida Munnetra Kazhagam (AIADMK) leader's first and immensely successful bid to become chief minister of Tamil Nadu for the first time since the demise of her mentor, the iconic former chief minister of Tamil Nadu, M.G. Ramachandran, MGR.

But in an odd twist of fate that evening, I went from Jayalalitha's Poes Garden house to the headquarters of the Dravida Munnetra Kazhagam (DMK) and then to the Congress chief's office. At the DMK headquarters, the topic of discussion was how much of a threat Jayalalitha posed to the party, and how the Congress must be cut to size as every pre-poll survey indicated that the Congress, pitted against a divided Opposition, wouldn't do too badly nationally. At the Congress party office I met with the then Tamil Nadu Congress Committee head, Vazhapadi Ramamurthy.

There had been stray incidents of violence throughout the day in the city. Without much prompting, Vazhapadi warned me that he had heard from the grapevine there would be violence the next day as well, while confirming, to my great excitement, that Rajiv Gandhi was indeed arriving late the next night and would most probably address a rally, not far from Madras at Sriperumbudur.

Whether he was hinting that there would be some kind of violence at Rajiv Gandhi's rally or not, I have never been able to fathom—and I've replayed that conversation in my head a zillion times over. Could he have been warning me off? What did he know? After all, Vazhapadi was the first—and only—person to talk, a full twenty-four hours before the assassination, of the dangers posed by the Sri Lankan Tamils who were based in sizeable numbers in Madras and how their very presence in the city and the state was not conducive to peace or safety.

The warning was couched in the vaguest of terms, and it was only when I was sending off my report on the assassination that I remembered what he had said, connected the dots and wove it into the story, thereby becoming one of the first reporters to point fingers at the Liberation Tigers of Tamil Eelam (LTTE) as the possible perpetrators. Moments after the assassination, on the night of 21 May, one of the senior officers of the Madras police I had accosted at Sriperumbudur had raised the involvement of the Tigers as a distinct possibility. In fact, unbeknownst to most people in authority, and without even knowing for certain if the LTTE was involved, the Madras police had begun rounding up Sri Lankan students of Tamil origin and throwing them into jail.

Years later, Ravindran, the manager of the Tamil newspaper *Virakesari* in Jaffna, Sri Lanka, would tell me how he never managed to finish his engineering degree because of that one night when he was arrested and kept in a Madras jail for a few days, before he hot-footed it back home.

~

A commercial pilot before he entered politics, Rajiv Gandhi had flown his own plane from Visakhapatnam where he had addressed a rally earlier that evening for Congress candidate Uma Gajapathi Raju.

Sriperumbudur would have been called off in all likelihood had Rajiv Gandhi's plane, which had developed technical problems in Visakhapatnam, not been fixed at the very last minute.

Hundreds of supporters lined the streets all the way to Sriperumbudur on the bumpy, narrow road from Madras. Every time the car slowed and the crowd pushed forward, people would reach through the open window and pinch his cheek!

En route to Sriperumbudur and then again as we turned into the rally grounds, something struck me—security for the former prime minister, virtually non-existent after prime ministers V.P. Singh and Chandrashekhar had withdrawn his Z security, could open the door to an attack of some kind.

There was a sea of flags fluttering from the poles that ringed the rally venue and a podium at the far end. But unlike other poll rallies where there was a clear demarcation between the VIP area and the seating area for the audience, there was just open ground with a few hundred people milling about within the bamboo barricades, shouting slogans. The lighting was extremely poor. Most of the place was in darkness as the former prime minister's car approached. Someone had clearly skimped on the arrangements when the venue of the rally was shifted from the local college to the temple grounds. And I said so.

In my mind's eye, I can still see Rajiv Gandhi's gentle smile that showed not the slightest irritation at the less than conducive arrangements at the rally venue. I can still hear his voice as he turned his head and half-jokingly asked local member of Parliament Margatham Chandrashekhar who was sitting in the back seat of the car where I was, kneeling, wedged uncomfortably into the tiny space between the driver and Rajiv Gandhi, 'Did you hear what Neena just said, Margatham? Why are there no lights? Why is it so dimly lit? There seem to be very few people. Where are your supporters? This doesn't seem like an election rally at all . . .' Half-joking or not, he wasn't far off the mark.

The government's inexplicable scrapping of Rajiv Gandhi's security even though the Congress leader's life was under threat had set Lutyens' Delhi speculating on whether there was more to the move than met the eye, and had laid him wide open and vulnerable to attack.

Given the family's recent history of deaths and assassinations, the removal of the Black Cats cover didn't make sense. Rajiv Gandhi's younger brother, Sanjay, had died under mysterious circumstances in a plane crash in 1980, with speculation rife that the two-seater aircraft had been sabotaged, while his mother, the indomitable Indira Gandhi had been gunned down in 1984 by her own Sikh bodyguards who had been reinstated against the explicit instructions of intelligence agencies.

As the car in which we were travelling hit yet another pothole, a group of slogan-shouting supporters tried to grab him through the open window. He was even lit up like a beacon, with a light fixture above the windscreen focused directly on him. There was little doubt that at one level, Rajiv Gandhi saw the mass hysteria wherever he went as a sign of his immense popularity, as a vindication that the people still loved him and that he remained his party's main vote-catcher. But at some level, he was concerned. While nobody could have predicted that his life would be snuffed out just like that only minutes later, he had an almost prescient premonition of his own death.

Unsettled by the complete absence of security— no gunman would have been able to protect him, had someone lunged at him through the open window with a knife or taken a shot at him—I had asked him, pointedly, whether he felt his life was at risk, more so now that there was absolutely no security beyond the one token bodyguard, who was, incidentally, in another car.

Rajiv Gandhi responded with a counter-question: 'Have you noticed how every time any South Asian leader of any import rises to a position of power or is about to achieve something for himself or his country, he is cut down, attacked, killed . . . look at Mrs [Indira] Gandhi, Sheikh Mujib, look at Zulfikar Ali Bhutto, at Zia-ul-Haq, Bandaranaike . . .'

Within minutes of making that bone-chilling prophetic statement that hinted there were dark forces at work and that he knew he was a target, Rajiv Gandhi himself would be gone.

~

As we turned off the main road, there was a mandatory burst of welcoming firecrackers. We had stopped on a slope on slightly higher ground and had walked down the approach, a few hundred yards or so to the open space in front of the main temple at Sriperumbudur, where a red carpet had been laid out.

Stepping out from the front seat, Rajiv Gandhi had said, 'Come, come, follow me,' and I had demurred, walking to the back and around and then to the front of the car so I could have a bird's-eye view of the venue, without having to deal with the throng.

'I have one more question,' I had said. 'I'll wait for you here.'

A bomb, a suicide bomber, let alone the first female suicide bomber on Indian soil, was the last thing on anyone's mind as Rajiv Gandhi plunged into the crowd of supporters on his way to the podium at the far side of the ground, shaking hands, smiling warmly, as was his wont, at everyone who reached out to him.

But as the huge explosion went off a few minutes later and I, standing about ten steps away, felt what I later realized was blood and gore from the victims splatter all over my arms and my white sari, a nameless dread took hold—something terrible had happened to the man I had just been talking with.

The last time I had followed Rajiv Gandhi into a crowd had been exactly two years earlier, in 1989, in Kalwakurthy, the constituency of the Andhra Pradesh chief minister, the larger-than-life N.T. Rama Rao, where Rajiv Gandhi was set to campaign.

Back then, we had driven in what had seemed like an endless 100-car cavalcade, complete with Black Cat commandos and top security, all the way from Hyderabad to the venue. As I got out to follow Rajiv Gandhi, a wave of people converged around the Congress leader who was surrounded by bodyguards, even as I was knocked into a narrow little ditch. Unable to move for several minutes, and out for the count, I sensed rather than saw dozens of people jumping over me.

This time, I was deeply reluctant to follow Rajiv Gandhi into the crowd.

At Sriperumbudur, he had no such compunctions. Minutes after he walked unhesitatingly into the crowd, there was a deafening sound as the bomb spluttered to life and exploded in a blinding flash. Everything changed.

A moment that, in my head, will always be frozen in time. It was exactly 10.21 p.m.

~

Months earlier, in February 1991, while covering the first Gulf War and the liberation of Kuwait by Allied Forces and NATO, I had walked the beaches of Kuwait with a team of French de-miners. I had a fair knowledge of what bombs looked and sounded like. Except, the French kept you at a safe distance, out of harm's way, and insisted you use the earplugs they provided when they detonated the Claymore mines.

Who saw Sriperumbudur coming . . .

So when the suicide bomber did set off her bomb, the first thing I said to Suman Dubey, Rajiv Gandhi's media adviser—I had stopped to talk to him instead of following Rajiv Gandhi into the crowd—was that this was no ordinary blast, quickly correcting my first reaction as I scanned the scene in front of me, from 'That sounds like a very odd firecracker' to 'No, no, that's definitely a bomb.'

The silence once the bomb went off must have lasted less than a fraction of a second. But that moment, until all hell broke loose, the shrieks and the wailing, was the stuff of nightmares. None of the war coverage I had done in Kuwait or Iraq had prepared me for this. Every single person ahead of me had died in the blast. Bits of their clothing had been seared on to their bodies, but most of it had been burnt off. Their exposed flesh looked as if it had been roasted, blackened. It was a grisly sight. Raw, still bleeding from their wounds, many lay face up, a mangled mass of tangled bodies. Dead people. There were headless torsos, body parts, arms and legs . . . Some were barely alive; many were dying, stacked up against the grisly dead. It was macabre, a scene from hell.

As the panicked crowd around me and on the other side of the scene took to their heels, the people screaming as they came running up, some coming straight at me as I tried to move towards the site of the blast, I was shoved this way and that. As they ran past, and in all directions, a part of me noted that many were police and security personnel. In the ensuing melee, few cared that as they pushed aside the flimsy bamboo barricades and broke through the rows of chairs, they were stepping over a clutch of the freshly dead.

Gone was the excited crowd that had been shouting and cheering only seconds before. In its place were the wails, the screams, as I ran forward; and then, someone behind me pulled me back just in time and said in Tamil, 'Watch out, you're about to step on somebody's arm.' The revulsion, the horror was complete.

As I fought my way through to the blast site that was only a few feet away, stepping over the debris of the dead and the broken barricades, the one thought running through my head was the fate of Rajiv Gandhi. He was in there somewhere in that mass of bodies. How serious was it? Could he have survived it? Could he be *dead*?

And then I saw his body. It was a sight I would never forget.

'Why is he just lying there? Why doesn't someone help him up? Someone should get him to a hospital, get him immediate emergency treatment . . . Where is the emergency medical team? Has someone called the hospital?' I said out loud. No one was listening.

The next, and far more selfish, jumble of thoughts that crowded in was how to get out of there. I had to find the driver of my car. I had no idea where he was.

After we left the Meenambakam airport earlier that evening, the cavalcade accompanying Rajiv Gandhi had slowed down at the turnoff from the Grand Southern Trunk Road to the 25-kilometre drive to Sriperumbudur.

A man, clearly a security guard, was moving steadily down the line of cars, peering into each car and asking something. He reached my car and asked, 'Neena Gopal?' When I said 'Yes', he gestured for me to follow him. I guessed I was finally getting the interview with the man who every pre-poll survey predicted would be the next prime minister and, in my excitement, I left my camera and my handbag—and all the cash I had—in my car, telling the driver to stay close and come looking for me when we stopped. In the aftermath of the blast, without having any way of communicating with the driver who may well have fled too, I knew I was stranded. How was I going to get back to Madras to file the story? How long would it take to get from here to the city? Where was the nearest telephone? How was I going to tell my editors at *Gulf News*, Dubai, in the United Arab Emirates where I was based, that I had just witnessed the gory end of one of India's most beloved leaders?

~

As the terrified crowd fled from the spot where the dead and injured lay, and bewildered, anxious survivors ran through the gathering throng in the semi-darkness, I spotted Congress leaders G.K. Moopanar and Jayanti Natarajan, and Margatham who had been in the car with me, and at whose behest the former prime minister had made a special effort to address this oddly timed, late-night election rally.

They looked shaken, aghast, devastated at the sight of Rajiv Gandhi's prone, seemingly lifeless body. Margatham looked shattered, as if her world had ended. Rajiv Gandhi had only come to Sriperumbudur at 'Aunty's' request.

The next day both Natarajan and Moopanar would separately tell me how they had tried to lift Rajiv Gandhi from the ground but couldn't as his body 'simply disintegrated in their hands'. Worse, how at that crucial moment, they couldn't find a single policeman, barring Rajiv Gandhi's personal bodyguard, Pradip Kumar Gupta (the man who had come looking for me), who was lying right next to Rajiv Gandhi and had died in the blast.

There was no ambulance—now an accepted fixture at election rallies. They couldn't find any medical personnel, or a stretcher or gurney or even a vehicle to get him to the nearest hospital. In fact, within minutes of the blast, two cars, one a white Ambassador flashing a red beacon, and another that came from somewhere in the back, had backed on to the main road and sped away.

The mood on the ground was getting decidedly ugly. At the spot where Rajiv Gandhi's body lay, it was getting more and more difficult to hold one's ground as his supporters closed in, muttering unintelligibly under their breath. The undercurrent of anger and hostility was palpable, as the party workers at the ill-chosen venue began to shout

'*Vazhige Rajiv Gandhi! Vazhige!* (Long live Rajiv Gandhi! Long live!),' not knowing, perhaps, how inappropriate a slogan it was. It was apparent they were still looking for some way to vent their fury, and were only holding back from heading out and smashing everything around them because it was unclear what exactly had happened to Rajiv Gandhi—whether he was dead or grievously injured, and who exactly was behind the blast.

It was the DMK, said one man with great certainty. 'Kalaingar' (the moniker for Muthuvel Karunanidhi) hated Rajiv Gandhi and had openly said that he must be stopped. His words elicited loud murmurs of support from the throng of Congress workers, until another man said it wasn't the DMK at all and was promptly slapped and pushed around. Nobody was thinking straight. As Rajiv Gandhi lay there, and Moopanar tried to keep the throng at bay, the crowd was vocalizing what was going through all our minds.

One man kept insisting that Rajiv Gandhi had survived the blast; that he was only injured and all that was required was for someone, anyone, to take him to the nearby hospital. Many concurred. None of them could even countenance the prospect that he had breathed his last, as the tearful crowds kept saying '*Paapa, rosa poo maadhiriyirikidai* (Poor man, he looks like a rose),' a reference to Rajiv Gandhi's fair skin.

No one could say the unsayable.

From the corner of my eye, I finally saw a vehicle that I presumed was an ambulance, lights flashing, trying to make its way from the main road that we had left only minutes earlier. Blocked by the crowd, it was inching its way forward. I had to move with it, follow the ambulance carrying Rajiv Gandhi's body, take the story to its logical conclusion.

By a stroke of luck, as I was pushing my way through the crowd, trying to find the car that I had hired for the evening, Rajiv Gandhi's driver emerged from the melee. I didn't know him personally but he called out to me and said he had been looking for me everywhere. Catching me by the arm, he said, 'We should leave; it's not safe here. Anything can happen. Let's go, let's go, I will take you back to Madras. Once the protests start, there will be riots, they will block all the roads; we won't be able to get back.'

Brushing aside my protests about abandoning the Congress leaders if we left, and how we should stay with Rajiv Gandhi's body, he insisted that I go with him, assuring me we would follow the body, which we were anyway ill-equipped to transport. With no sign of my driver and realizing this was my only way back to the city, I jumped in as he quickly reversed the car. We inched our way out of the venue as I continued to scan the scene for my driver who was nowhere to be found.

We followed the ambulance to a hospital just ahead; checked whether Rajiv Gandhi's body would be kept there overnight and, receiving conflicting, contradictory reports from the bewildered medical personnel there, with no one ready to confirm or deny that he had indeed died, we raced to Madras before the mobs had a chance to block the roads into the city.

At the Central Telegraph Office on Mount Road, as I typed the copy, for once the sleepy telex operators were all awake. They stood behind me, their jaws dropping, reading the story as I wrote it.

Rajiv Gandhi was dead. Assassinated at 10.21 p.m. on 21 May 1991.

~

Once I filed the story and returned to my uncle-in-law's apartment on Harrington Road in Madras, where I was staying, I fielded telephone calls from my anxious family, particularly my husband, who said that the minute he saw the news of the assassination on television in Dubai, he was certain in his heart that I was there! I spoke to our daughter, Shwetha, who was not yet ten at the time. Blissfully unaware of how close I had come to being blown up, she happily poured out the travails of her day at school as I sounded determinedly cheerful, while making a mental note that she needed a brother or a sister and should not be alone. Our second daughter, Sharada, would be born just over nine months later, a precious pregnancy that would have me confined to the bed till she was born.

My husband's wonderful uncle, M.K. Ramdas, was fielding all the other calls, including the critical one from his cousin M.K. Narayanan (who was also my husband's uncle). Narayanan headed the Intelligence Bureau (IB) and wanted every single detail of the night's terrible events. He listened patiently as I described what I had seen, asking me repeatedly about the ring of fire that I insisted I had seen around Rajiv Gandhi as he lay on the ground, minutes after the bomb had exploded. Only much later would it hit me that if there was indeed a ring of flames around the blast site, it would imply the use of landmines.

The next morning, an IB team assigned by Narayanan came to hear my account after they had reconnoitred the Sriperumbudur area. They said they saw no evidence of a ring of fire but conceded that what I had seen must have been the flames when the victims' possessions and clothes caught fire. They listened as I described the shocking lack of security for a former prime minister who had only four years earlier survived an assassination attempt in Colombo by a Sri Lankan naval rating.

Even at that point, as we mourned the death of a wonderfully warm human being, few had a clue about who was actually responsible for the killing. The investigators hadn't yet gone public with the fact that a senior policeman and his team had stumbled upon a camera that had captured telling images of Rajiv Gandhi's assassins.

I was in limbo, in some sort of a bubble. In shock. It was only when I got back to my parents' home in Bangalore (now Bengaluru) and my normally undemonstrative parents enveloped me in a highly unusual bear hug that I began to shiver uncontrollably and allowed myself to cry and mourn the passing of Rajiv Gandhi. The full horror of what I had witnessed, and the images and emotions that I had blocked and suppressed for seventy-two hours came rushing back.

~

On 24 May, the nation stayed riveted to television screens as the funeral, attended by dignitaries from over sixty countries, was telecast live. The mortal remains of Rajiv Gandhi were consigned to flames on the banks of the Yamuna; his stoic son, Rahul, and daughter, Priyanka, the cynosure of all eyes.

Days later, I received a call from the Indian embassy in Abu Dhabi. Rajiv Gandhi's widow had sent a message asking me to meet her at their New Delhi home at 10, Janpath. I flew to Delhi on 31 May and, as I walked from the Congress party office to the pathway that led to the house that Rajiv Gandhi had called home, alongside the Gandhi man-Friday V. George, I was accosted by several senior Congressmen, saying I must find out at any cost, whether Sonia Gandhi would lead the Congress party!

Inside, in a room lined with books and a long table where Rajiv Gandhi had often been photographed confabulating with his cabinet, was Sonia Gandhi, her face devoid of make-up, a far cry from the beautifully coiffed creature whom I had met on her visit to Dubai a few months ago. She reached across, held both my hands in hers and said, 'Tell me everything, tell me what he said, what mood was he in, what were his last moments like. I want to hear it from you, every tiny detail. Was he happy, was he tense, what were his last words . . .'

Tears streaming down her cheeks—and, I realized, mine too—and still holding on to my hands, she listened as I recounted the last forty-five minutes of India's youngest prime minister's life; his unexpected death closing the chapter on India's all too brief Camelot.

2

The Hunt for the Assassins

IF R.K. RAGHAVAN, INSPECTOR GENERAL of police in charge of security at Sriperumbudur, hadn't stumbled upon a camera sitting atop a dead man in the aftermath of the blast, the story of the probe into the assassination of Rajiv Gandhi would have been very different.

The object of much scorn in the media for the two low points in his career: the probe into the 2002 Godhra riots that exonerated Narendra Modi and—just over a decade before that—the appallingly poor security at Rajiv Gandhi's election rally at Sriperumbudur on 21 May 1991, Raghavan found a vital piece of evidence that set investigators on the path to hunting down Rajiv Gandhi's assassins.

No one knew if the camera had recorded Rajiv Gandhi's last moments, least of all, the explosion that claimed the life of a promising leader and the eighteen others who died with him. Not until the film in the camera was examined within forty-eight hours of the assassination and the first prints were taken—there were ten photographs in all—were investigators able to zero in on the probable killers.

Two people stood out in the crowd: a dark, stocky young woman in an all-enveloping salwar-kameez and a short man in a crumpled, ill-fitting, white kurta-pyjama.

The black-and-white frames—originally in colour—would unravel the shocking conspiracy behind an assassination that only the Mahatma's and Indira Gandhi's could rival in this country for the tag, 'assassination of the century'.

The photographs gave the LTTE no room for plausible deniability; the terror outfit was responsible for unleashing their *karampuli*, a Black Tigress, on their unsuspecting, first foreign target.

Without the camera, it might have been just another 'blind case'. Unsolved. Unresolved. Never laid to rest.

~

As the blast ripped through Rajiv Gandhi's upper body and threw him face down on the stony outcrop of land near the VIP area, Raghavan was barely a few feet away. He recalls how smoke from the bomb temporarily blinded him. 'I couldn't see anything. I lost my vision for several minutes after the blast. It was all a blur.'

As people began screaming and running in all directions, Raghavan pushed his way towards where the

Congress leader had been standing—the spot that should have been a sanitized security zone but had been breached in spectacular fashion within minutes of his arrival.

Despite the threat perception that the former prime minister faced, Raghavan claims he hadn't factored in the possibility that the target could be Rajiv Gandhi. 'But the minute it hit me that it could be him, that he could have died, then like a madcap (sic) I began shouting for him, by name, hoping he would answer and my fears would be unfounded . . . until, we, Moopanar and I, and Vazhapadi Ramamurthy who came running from the dais, finally found him.' In fact, Raghavan became the first person to inspect the shell which was all that was left of Rajiv Gandhi's broken body. (Moopanar was the former Tamil Nadu Congress Committee [TNCC] chief; Vazhapadi, the serving one.)

As policemen and political workers alike ran for cover, fearing more bombs would go off, Raghavan stood his ground, determined to protect the scene of the crime.

The top cop and his team had inspected the venue of the rally in Tamil Nadu MP Margatham's constituency soon after they had been alerted that Rajiv Gandhi was coming. First, on 20 May, a day before the former prime minister was to arrive from Hyderabad, and again on 21 May, as early as 5 p.m. that evening.

'We didn't expect any problems that day, none at all,' he says, although he admits that, given the kind of threat he was under, 'security for Rajiv Gandhi wasn't at the level that it should have been'. Curiously, neither former Central Bureau of Investigation (CBI) Joint Director and Inspector General D.R. Kaarthikeyan who was given charge of a Special Investigation Team (SIT) within hours, nor the Commission of Inquiry set up on 27 May under Justice J.S. Verma, would prosecute the men responsible for these lapses.

The onus of the security lapse lay as much with the Congress party as with the local police, although with Margatham's pointman A.J. Doss browbeating the police into submission, the former was more to blame. Kaarthikeyan, in his book *The Rajiv Gandhi Assassination*,[1] writes of the overzealous Doss brushing aside concerns of policemen and TNCC officials, and insisting on clearing a host of people who were given access to Rajiv Gandhi—twenty-three in all—that night. The list included a Congress worker named Latha Kannan who was given top clearance because of her proximity to Margatham; Latha would prove crucial for the bomber to gain access to Rajiv Gandhi.

At the time, it wasn't de rigueur for women thronging election rallies to be screened, frisked or scanned with metal detectors. Even if the metal detectors had been set up at Sriperumbudur as police say they had, claiming they

---

[1] D.R. Kaarthikeyan, *Triumph of Truth, The Rajiv Gandhi Assassination: The Investigation* (New Delhi: Sterling Publishers, 2004).

had two metal detectors in place, the question of how a suicide bomber, weighed down with half a kilo of RDX, got through them has never been adequately addressed.

Doss's crossed wires with the police—and the TNCC—had him believing that the police would screen those twenty-three people. The police, on their part, thought it was Doss who should scrutinize the invitees. In the event, their collective failure to sanitize the VIP area, keep out people who had not been thoroughly vetted and position the barricades to keep the crowds at bay, was completely overlooked by the police top brass.

Raghavan, who had served in the SPG assigned to Rajiv Gandhi when he was prime minister, knew the drill and admits to the gaping holes in the security arrangements. 'I did see the gaps. I'd served in the SPG for Rajiv Gandhi ten times,' he says, but adds that there was nothing anyone could have done at that late hour.

Critically, in the confusion over whether or not the Congress leader would be travelling to Madras that night, his personal armed gunman stayed behind in Hyderabad, leaving the former premier with just one security guard, Pradip Kumar Gupta. Gupta, who perished in the blast, was standing right beside him when the bomb exploded.

Police negligence on the ground, combined with the fact that Doss was calling the shots, allowed the suicide bomber to quietly attach herself to party worker Latha and get close enough to Rajiv Gandhi to self-detonate.

But Raghavan assigns the blame elsewhere. He says that the person who should bear the primary responsibility for single-handedly removing the SPG cover that could have protected Rajiv Gandhi and thrown a security ring around him under exactly such circumstances, was former prime minister V.P. Singh. On succeeding Rajiv Gandhi as prime minister, the Raja scrapped SPG protection for former prime ministers, restricting it to serving prime ministers only.

'History will never forgive him,' says Raghavan of V.P. Singh. 'Nobody will.'

Neither the SIT nor subsequent commissions of inquiry held V.P. Singh to account. Nor, for that matter, were the men in charge of Rajiv Gandhi's security while he was in the state—the Tamil Nadu police and Doss—ever brought to book. (Rajiv Gandhi himself had famously brought the Chandrashekhar government down on the grounds that the government, using the security threat as a ploy to spy on his movements, had put him, his home and his phones under the surveillance of two constables from Haryana.)

Will history judge Raghavan more kindly? As he scoured the area looking for something, anything, to help him find out who had set off the explosion and what kind of bomb had been used, he says he espied the camera lying on a dead man.

'It had not been damaged at all, just covered with earth and grass,' he tells me, 'and I had absolutely no idea then of the significance of that camera. I picked it up, directed one of my men to secure it and keep it safe in the hope that there would be something there. I didn't know at the time if it did.'

Without that one crucial bit of evidence, the hunt for the assassins could have taken a different route. With it, the SIT was able to painstakingly track down all the killers, one by one, and bring them to justice.

~

In Black and White

On 23 May, *The Hindu* ran one of the photographs taken from the camera that Raghavan had retrieved and blew the case wide open. The new SIT head, Kaarthikeyan, says he hadn't even seen the original prints at that point. The film roll extracted from the camera had been given to the chief of the Tamil Nadu Forensic Science Laboratory (TNFSL). The TNFSL head who had arrived at the blast venue with the local reporter from *The Hindu* was given the camera, and the newspaper gained access to the crucial roll of film when it was developed.

The photograph shocked the world. There she was, Rajiv Gandhi's assassin—the first female suicide bomber. And yet no one could identify her, no one knew anything about her.

According to the SIT which swiftly went to work under Kaarthikeyan, apart from the ten frames, intelligence officials stumbled upon a video recording of the event by a music troupe that was entertaining the crowd that evening. It showed the same bespectacled young woman, dressed in an orange salwar-kameez, inching her way forward, trying to get close to the former premier. The outfit, favoured by women from the north and rarely worn by Tamil girls at the time, caught the attention of the then IB chief Narayanan as well. (Controversially, no recording of that video was subsequently seen or submitted as evidence and there are unconfirmed reports that the pertinent section of the video, when it did turn up, turned out to be blank.)

Either way, this woman was unknown, an outsider. Who was she? Who was the man in white in the far corner of one of the other pictures? He had been cropped out of the photograph published by *The Hindu* because, as the newspaper's editor N. Ram later told the SIT, he could have been a journalist. What was their connection to the assassination? Neither of them was a Congress party worker. What business did they have that night at Sriperumbudur?

Within a day came the post-mortem on Rajiv Gandhi, which said he had 'multiple penetrating wounds', twenty-two injuries; part of his face, skull and most of his brain had been completely destroyed, and his badly mutilated upper body peppered with pellets.

The CBI, says K. Ragothaman, one of its officers seconded to Kaarthikeyan's SIT, had meanwhile sent the mutilated body parts of the hitherto unidentified woman found at the blast site for a DNA test to the Centre for Cellular and Molecular Biology in Hyderabad. Her face was still recognizable, Ragothaman says. 'I can recall it like it was yesterday. She was the only one among the people who died in the blast that night whose body had been so completely dismembered.'

'Her head had been severed from her body and was lying at a distance of 12 metres; her upper body cleaved in two, was in shreds, her right arm blown off, her left arm lying further away and both her legs were in separate pieces,' he said. Like Rajiv Gandhi's body, and those of all the other victims, hers too, bore strikingly similar pellet marks and burns.

(The TNFSL chief, in fact, was pulled up by the SIT in their final report for ordering hospital staff to reattach the assassin's decapitated head to her body.)

The forensics teams from the Central Forensic Science Laboratory, the TNFSL and explosives experts from the National Security Guard (NSG) who swept the scene on 23 May and gathered the first pieces of material evidence found that hundreds of metallic pellets lay littered at the spot. Among the debris of human body parts lay wires, two toggle switches and overwhelming evidence of the explosive RDX.

The woman whose body was found closest to Rajiv Gandhi's had been wearing an undergarment that was part vest, part belt. Experts piecing it together from the blood-soaked shreds discovered on the burnt-out red carpet, found that it was made of blue denim on the outside and on the inside. It had electric wires running through insulation sleeves concealed in the inner layer to support a slab of RDX that probably weighed half a kilo and was embedded with 10,000 pellets. This was integral to the ingeniously constructed Improvised Explosive Device (IED) that the human bomb was strapped to.

The team of experts found that electric detonators plugged into the slab were connected to a 9-volt Golden Power battery through two switches—one to arm the device, the other to set it off.

'On detonation, apart from the sound, fire and blast effect, the thousands of pellets would become projectiles or shrapnel travelling at furious speed, destroying everything in their immediate path,' says Kaarthikeyan in his compelling book co-written with the late CBI officer Deputy Inspector General Radhavinod Raju.

Rajiv Gandhi didn't stand a chance. Nobody within 10 feet of the first human bomb on Indian soil did. Those of us on the periphery only survived because of the dense crowd around the Congress leader, which bore the brunt of the blast.

Two things happened in quick succession after *The Hindu* published the picture of the human bomb.

One, Kaarthikeyan's investigative team which was able to connect the dots with incredible precision, filing their charge sheet within the year, accessed a policewoman, the eyewitness Sub-Inspector Anasuya who had survived the blast that had burnt part of her face and blown off three fingers. When shown the photographs, she confirmed that she had seen both the bespectacled woman and the man in the white kurta, as well as the young photographer, who had been hanging around, standing by the red carpet just before Rajiv Gandhi's arrival.

Secondly, after *The Hindu* published the picture of the dead photographer, from whose camera the tell-all images had been retrieved, he was identified as Haribabu by a journalist who knew him. The journalist also made a very interesting revelation. He told Kaarthikeyan's team that Haribabu had introduced the man in the kurta-pyjama to him as the business partner of another photo-journalist they both knew.

His suspicions aroused, the journalist called the photo-journalist the next day to verify the story. While the latter freely admitted that he had let Haribabu borrow his Chinon camera, he categorically denied knowing the kurta-clad man in the picture, who Haribabu had claimed was his (the photojournalist's) business partner. The journalist alerted the SIT.

Critically, Mr 'White Kurta' was not found among the dead or the injured. He was still at large. The SIT wasn't sure if he was acquainted with the woman standing next to him, or whether they both were part of the team of assassins.

The identification of Haribabu led to another lead that, for the first time, reinforced Kaarthikeyan's own suspicions about the involvement of the LTTE terror group. Kaarthikeyan's team discovered that Haribabu worked closely with another photographer, Subha Sundaram, who had pro-LTTE leanings and had famously played host to the Madras-based Tiger operative 'Baby' Subramaniam and many other LTTE sympathizers at his Studio Shubha.

That's when the finger of suspicion first pointed to the Tigers, who, until then, had only been tagged—as had the Khalistan Sikhs, the United Liberation Front of Asom (ULFA) and Kashmiri extremists—as one of the many groups that had an axe to grind against Rajiv Gandhi and his family.

At this point, the SIT concluded that Haribabu, an LTTE sympathizer, had been contracted to film the assassination—the LTTE was known to record everything—and possibly had stood too close to the female bomber and died accidentally in the blast.

The IB came to much the same conclusion after an exhaustive review of the history of bomb blasts in Tamil Nadu perpetrated by the LTTE and other Sri Lankan Tamil militants in the southern state when the DMK government had been in power but had looked the other way, giving the Tigers a free run. The IB ruled out the Sikhs, given the logistics involved—organizing a hit from their area of operations in the north would have been impossible.

The Research and Analysis Wing (RAW) had a much harder time arriving at the same conclusion, given their long association with the militants and the 'moles' they cultivated within the Tiger ranks who played both sides with ease. The London-based Col Kittu (real name Sathasivan Krishnakumar), for instance, was one of the people on RAW's rolls, as maverick politician Subramanian Swamy says in his book, *The Assassination of Rajiv Gandhi*.[2]

∼

Soon after the assassination, Kaarthikeyan and CBI chief Vijay Karan left for Colombo on 30 May in a bid to see if the kurta-clad man in the photo and the woman bomber could be identified by Lankan Tamil groups inimical to the LTTE. At the same time, SIT sleuths began scrutinizing the various assassinations in Madras that had the LTTE's imprimatur.

Of major interest was the 19 June 1990 death squad, and the methods and weaponry they had used to savage and kill the Eelam People's Revolutionary Liberation

---

[2] Subramanian Swamy, *The Assassination of Rajiv Gandhi: Unanswered Questions and Unasked Queries* (New Delhi: Konark Publishers, 2000).

Front (EPRLF) leader K. Padmanabha and thirteen others with him at his office-cum-residence in Zacharia Colony in Kodambakkam, Madras. The killers had used grenades and AK-47s, and not a belt-bomb. Nevertheless, SIT sleuths saw how the solid wooden door of the apartment had been blasted open with grenades, and how the metallic pellets that were embedded in it replicated the ones found in the assassin's belt-bomb.

One of the grenades used in the EPRLF attack, which had not exploded, had both RDX and TNT, and contained 2800 pellets. The SIT was briefed that the grenade, which bore the stamp 'SFG-87' that stood for Singapore Fragmentation Grenade-87, had been manufactured by Chartered Industries of Singapore. The similarities were striking, but despite their efforts, Indian intelligence had been unable to identify Padmanabha's killers. They had the names—David or Robert and Raghuvaran—but with no pictures and no identikit, it was impossible for the SIT to link the two killings or pin it on the LTTE.

On 30 May, there was another tip-off from a resident of Villivakam colony in Madras. He said he recognized the woman in the green salwar-kameez. He had seen her when she visited his new neighbour, a woman called Nalini, along with another woman and a man, who had been introduced to him as Das. He knew Nalini was employed in an office in Adyar but had not seen her of late.

In the first week of June, the SIT hit a mother lode when it unearthed a boxful of papers, letters and bills while searching Haribabu's home in a Madras slum. The documents showed the extent of Haribabu's involvement with the separatists. Haribabu's father gave the SIT more boxes, one of which contained bills for the sandalwood garland that the bomber was holding when she approached Rajiv Gandhi. Other boxes revealed a chit that had Nalini's and Das's names on it, a telephone number and 3000 copies of an LTTE-compiled book called *Satanic Forces*, which was a collection of articles and opinion pieces that rained hate on the Indian Peace Keeping Force (IPKF) and India's Sri Lanka policy. As SIT investigator K. Ragothaman and author of *Conspiracy to Kill Rajiv Gandhi from CBI Files*[3] recounts, the book was an eye-opener—the LTTE's loathing for Rajiv Gandhi was its one recurring, chilling leitmotif.

The final tip-off that would blow the lid off the LTTE conspiracy came when the photojournalist with whom Haribabu worked gave the SIT the name of the printer who had printed all the pro-LTTE material—Bhagyanathan. In him, they found the one source who would uncover the elaborate LTTE network of drivers, smugglers, supporters and spies that operated right under their noses across the state.

---

[3] K. Ragothaman, *Conspiracy to Kill Rajiv Gandhi from CBI Files* (New Delhi: Manas Publications, 2013).

Apprehended and brought in for questioning, the twenty-five-year-old Bhagyanathan was being interrogated at the SIT headquarters, when a female witness who had come forward and who had been present at the rally that night, confirmed that the two women in Haribabu's pictures had been with Haribabu, the man in the kurta-pyjama and the human bomber, at the venue. She didn't know their names or antecedents but said they were all together as one team.

What followed in quick succession can only be described as a series of fortuitous coincidences.

One of the sleuths interrogating Bhagyanathan at Malligai, the building from which the SIT was operating in Madras, was asked to come and see the pictures that the witness was being shown, only for him to realize that he was looking at Bhagyanathan's sister Nalini, whom he had seen in the printer's home but not approached as he had had no cause to at the time.

Because of the chit of paper bearing her name that had been found in Haribabu's box—which the SIT had widely publicized—Nalini had already been questioned by her employer. Thereafter, she had vanished. Her employer said she resigned on 9 June.

Nalini's complicity in the Rajiv Gandhi assassination was never in doubt for the SIT investigators. According to Bhagyanathan, he, as well as his mother, Padma, who was a nurse, and his sister, Nalini, had taken under their wing two women who had been brought from Jaffna and entrusted to their care by a man they only knew as Raghu Anna. Nalini even helped the suicide bomber pick out and buy the oversized salwar-kameez on the morning of 21 May. It was while the young woman was getting ready that her LTTE female companion confirmed to Nalini that the man they intended to assassinate that night was Rajiv Gandhi—and not Annamalai Varadaraja Perumal, the first chief minister of Sri Lanka's North-Eastern Province and leader of the EPRLF as everyone had thought—and reportedly asked her to join them and watch history being made.

Nalini, au fait with the plan to eliminate the popular Indian leader, had already participated in a dry run with the gang of would-be assassins on 7 May 1991 during V.P. Singh's election rally in Madras. She had no qualms about going along to the 'real' thing. No longer an innocent bystander, more so as she had grown close to Das, she had attended office the day after the assassination as though nothing had happened, and did so every day until her boss confronted her on 9 June. After that, she never went back.

By 4 June, Kaarthikeyan and his team had returned from Colombo—summoned back by the RAW chief— with a list of the who's who of the vast LTTE network in Tamil Nadu that was a virtual state within a state.

Indeed, in January 1991, after the fall of the pro-LTTE DMK government, a crackdown on LTTE operatives and their supporters had been wrongly surmised as successful.

It was only when the SIT gained access to the list of Sri Lankan Tamils who had legally registered as foreign residents—while simultaneously tracking all the illegals, unearthing arms caches, wireless sets and huge amounts of cash—that the extent of the link between the mainland and the northern parts of the island, and the support they enjoyed, became clear.

Critically, Kaarthikeyan had returned from Colombo with the all-important name of the kurta-clad man. He was known by a string of aliases—Sivaraja Master, aka Sivaresan, real name Pakiachandran, nickname Paki or Kannadianna (meaning bespectacled older brother in Tamil) and Raghu Anna. The one-eyed LTTE operative was from Udippidy, Jaffna, with links to Batticaloa in the east.

Corroboration of his name came from the unlikeliest of sources. Just a day before the SIT chief's return, a smuggler caught doing the Sri Lankan run from the coastal village of Thiruthuraipoondi to Jaffna had independently identified the kurta-clad man as the one-eyed LTTE operative, Sivaresan.

In another major stroke of luck, Tamil Nadu Police stopped a young Sri Lankan Tamil speeding down a road near Vedaranyam on a motorcycle. When the SIT gained access to him, the man, Shankar, turned out to be part of the nine-member assassination squad under the command of Sivaresan, who had landed in the coastal village of Kodiakkarai, Nagapattinam, from Jaffna on 1 May 1991, along with the two women.

This was later corroborated by Shanmugham, an Indian smuggler from Kodiakkarai, whom the SIT nabbed based on the information that Shankar provided.

Shanmugham turned out to be one of the LTTE's key pointmen on the coast, the big fish who led them to the Tigers' secret stash of papers, photographs, videos, cyanide capsules, walkie-talkies and other equipment, as well as gold bars, cash and huge caches of guns and weapons.

As Ragothaman says, 'We collected thousands of photographs and videos of the LTTE training, one of which would finally help us home in on the identity of the human bomber and her handler.'

Much to the embarrassment of the SIT, however, Shanmugham committed suicide on their watch. With the benefit of hindsight, says Kaarthikeyan, leaving the smuggler in the company of his own uncle and in a police station that was close to his own home and that of his relatives—and his mistress—was a poor move. 'We don't know what transpired between Shanmugham and his uncle, but it led him to try to escape, and when he received no help from his relatives and the neighbours, he committed suicide,' the veteran investigator said.

Shanmugham had been working closely with the LTTE from Kodiakkarai since 1984, smuggling in people and arms under the cover of darkness. He had brought in the LTTE hit team that bumped off Padmanabha in 1990, and ensured their return to Jaffna once the job was done. Sivaresan was the head of that team.

Shankar, the LTTE operative, told the SIT about the nine-member hit squad that Shanmugham personally received at Kodiakkarai on 1 May. It included Sivaresan, as well as a one-legged man brought for treatment at one of the three hospitals in the state that fitted wounded Tigers with the Jaipur leg on the quiet and who was believed to be the wireless operator of the Tigers' intel chief. Also on that boat was Sivaresan's right-hand man, Suthenthiraja; his own wireless operator, Nehru; two young women and three others, including Shankar.

The interrogation of Shankar not only lifted the veil on the secret command structure of the Tigers in the state, it also led them to the various safe houses and hideouts where trained Sri Lankan Tamil assassins took shelter at the cash-rich Sivaresan's behest, leaving the SIT chief marvelling at the legions of sympathizers the LTTE could activate, particularly from the openly pro-LTTE cadres of the Dravida Kazhagam.

Most importantly, when he was caught, Shankar was carrying the office telephone number of Nalini—who, as wireless intercepts tracked by Indian sleuths revealed, was referred to as 'Office Girl'—and a contact number for Robert Payas, the local LTTE intelligence operative who worked with the hit squad during the operation. Payas had sent off the message that the assassination of Rajiv Gandhi, codenamed Operation Wedding, had been a success.

Bhagyanathan, when confronted with all of this, sang like a canary. He gave the SIT the full story, confirming Sivaresan's identity and that his real name was Raghuvaran or Raghu Anna. He also revealed that the one-eyed LTTE operative was the same man who had planned and executed Padmanabha's murder, which won him the unstinting praise and admiration of the outfit's chief, Vellupillai Prabhakaran, and resulted in his being entrusted with the onerous task of eliminating Rajiv Gandhi.

Bhagyanathan, young and impressionable, befriended by the LTTE's printer of propaganda, 'Baby' Subramanian, and another LTTE communications expert, Muthurajah, had quickly become part of the inner circle. But when questioned, he had little hesitation in naming the suicide bomber as Dhanu, her female companion as Subha, the possible standby bomber about whom very little is known, and the person who was seen in Nalini's company as Murugan alias Sriharan alias Das or Indu Master, who was Sivaresan's all-important Sri Lankan Tamil assistant and the explosives expert who helped build the belt-bomb.

The SIT finally had the who's who of Rajiv Gandhi's assassins.

Bhagyanathan also named several other Indian Tamils in thrall to the LTTE, including Arivu, real name Perarivalan, who would help Sivaresan buy the batteries that would power the belt-bomb that he and Murugan would construct, as well as a scooter and the wireless which Sivaresan used to communicate directly with Pottu Amman, the LTTE intelligence chief.

Three weeks into the investigation, the trail to Nalini and Murugan had gone cold. But, unfazed, on 11 June 1991, less than a month after the assassination, the SIT made its first formal arrests, detaining Bhagyanathan and his mother, Padma. There was no sign of 'One-eyed Jack' or, for that matter, the other woman caught on camera, Subha. But the SIT hoped they were closing in. Tracking down one LTTE operative after another who had been sent by Pottu Amman on the boat with Sivaresan saw all roads lead back to the mastermind. He was the spider in the web.

This is when the SIT stumbled upon another LTTE plot to assassinate a man whom the outfit had long seen as an Indian collaborator. While putting the final touches to the plan to eliminate the former Indian prime minister, Sivaresan was simultaneously trying to bring down Varadaraja Perumal, who had been installed in office much to Prabhakaran's chagrin when the IPKF had the LTTE with its back to the wall.

Sivaresan despatched an operative to Gwalior, where the EPRLF leader had taken refuge after the IPKF's retreat and

Rajiv Gandhi's electoral defeat in November 1989. But with Rajiv Gandhi's assassination and the mood against Sri Lankan Tamils turning ugly across the country, the LTTE operative he sent to Gwalior hot-footed it back to Tamil Nadu, hoping to meld in, only to be nabbed by the local police in Thanjavur. Varadaraja Perumal, the one man whom Sivaresan—and Prabhakaran and Pottu Amman—failed to eliminate.

And then, in the last week of June, the SIT would strike gold. While interrogating an LTTE operative, the SIT was told about the arrival in the last week of April 1991 of an old man named Sabapathy Pillai aka Kanakasabapathy Muthiah Sivaguranathan, whom Sivaresan wanted to ensconce in a Delhi house in Moti Bagh as part of his plan to attempt to assassinate Rajiv Gandhi in the capital, New Delhi. The Delhi house rented, Sabapathy, father of a slain LTTE commander of Jaffna, returned to the south to pick up his 'daughter-in-law' Athirai.

Oddly, despite the assassination of Rajiv Gandhi, Sabapathy and the girl were booked on a train back to Delhi on 1 July. The SIT, under the impression that the girl could be Subha, pulled out all the stops, arresting her and Sabapathy from a small hotel in Delhi.

She, however, wasn't Subha. But, as Ragothaman says, it was with the arrest of Athirai that the SIT investigators were finally able to tie up all the loose ends.

Athirai was Pottu Amman's Plan B. She was the alternate suicide bomber sent to assassinate Rajiv Gandhi in Delhi if Sivaresan's plan failed in Madras. After her arrest, Athirai, whose real name was Chandralekha but called herself Gowri or Sonia, would lay out the plot to assassinate Rajiv Gandhi in the greatest of detail to the SIT.

All the SIT needed now were the actual assassins—Sivaresan, Subha, Nalini and Murugan.

~

The Hunt for Sivaresan

Minutes after Dhanu blew herself up—after giving her mentor Sivaresan fair warning—Nalini, Subha and Sivaresan rushed to the Indira Gandhi statue just beyond the grounds and caught an autorickshaw into the city. They were heading to one of the many homes that LTTE sympathizers had lent them in Kodungaiyur, provided to them by an Indian Tamil who was married to a Lankan Tamil and had worked with the LTTE in various capacities. The next day, the group left for Tirupati, only returning to Madras on 26 May.

By then, with the photographs of Dhanu, Sivaresan and, later, Nalini published in the newspapers, the SIT began to get alerts from across the state that claimed they had been spotted. Sivaresan kept a low profile, rarely venturing out and putting up posters that were pro-Congress and pro-AIADMK to cover his tracks.

Most of the leads were dead ends. But in the case of Nalini and Murugan, the couple's luck ran out when they returned from Madurai to Madras and got spotted at the bus stand in Saidapet. They were formally arrested on 14 June. Nalini was pregnant with Murugan's child.

Kaarthikeyan, who interrogated them himself, says he was struck by her fiery, unrepentant defiance, her commitment to the LTTE, her strong conviction that the Tigers had been wronged, and her love for the younger man in her life, who was the father of her unborn child. Nalini, like her brother, Bhagyanathan, had no hesitation in owning up to the assassination, Kaarthikeyan said, although what her lawyers said in court would be an entirely different story.

More arrests quickly followed. The next to be nabbed was the hardcore Dravida Kazhagam activist and LTTE sympathizer Arivu aka Perarivalan—who helped put together the belt-bomb alongside Murugan—and Payas, who, along with his brother-in-law Jayakumar, were the LTTE's secret intelligence operatives in Madras.

Sivaresan was hiding in plain sight, in Eveready Colony in Kodungaiyur, using the home of an LTTE sympathizer, Vijayan, to send out short bursts from a wireless station that he had set up, which the SIT was unable to track despite their best efforts. A rogue radio station, only a stone's throw from the SIT's headquarters.

But nabbing Suthenthiraja, Sivaresan's most trusted assistant, after Athirai tipped them off on his hideout—

he was dragged from his bed before he could swallow his cyanide pill—was to prove one of the SIT's biggest coups and, certainly, Sivaresan's undoing. Not only could Sivaresan no longer bank on this key operative who outed their Kodungaiyur safe house, forcing him and Subha to flee, the young man would tell the SIT every last detail, conclusively implicating Sivaresan and the LTTE in Rajiv Gandhi's killing, and helping them prove the link with the 1990 killing of the EPRLF's Padmanabha.

Suthenthiraja aka Santhan was a neighbour of Sivaresan's from his village in Udippidy, and had known his boss as the son of an English teacher, Chandrashekharan Pillai of Veerabhadra Koiladdy. Suthenthiraja was a classmate of Sivaresan's younger brother, Ravichandran, who headed the Students Organization of the Liberation Tigers, and who probably died when he was taken into custody by the IPKF. Sivaresan, once an employee of the electricity board in Batticaloa, lost his eye in May 1987 in a clash with the Sri Lankan security forces and, some say, may even have been flown by the IPKF into Tamil Nadu for treatment.

That didn't change his loyalty to 'Thalapati', LTTE chief Prabhakaran, who picked him for three crucial hits— Padmanabha, Varadaraja Perumal and Rajiv Gandhi.

Suthenthiraja had been hand-picked and planted in Madras by Sivaresan in February 1990, to befriend and infiltrate the EPRLF's inner circle. It was the friendly young man's specific tip-off on a gathering of the EPRLF's top leadership to Sivaresan, giving him the exact time and place of the meeting, that led to the bloody attack on the Lankan Tamil group that Suthenthiraja participated in.

The politics of revenge that characterized the LTTE's brand of settling political scores, had been imported into India.

Based on the master list, courtesy a suspiciously co-operative Colombo under then President Ranasinghe Premadasa, members of Sivaresan's inner circle were being tracked down and nabbed, one by one. But the wily One-eyed Jack, Sivaresan, was always one step ahead of the SIT, proving to be far more elusive than they had anticipated.

~

Unleashing the Karampuli

Dhanu, the human suicide bomber, fascinated the sleuths. This was clearly not her real name, and the motivation and dedication that led her to take this path could only have come from sustained fanning of anti-India hatred from the LTTE's savvy propagandists such as Yogi and Prabhakaran himself.

Among the photographs, videos and cassettes that were seized by the SIT from Perarivalan and Bhagyanathan in their hunt for evidence to tie the LTTE to the assassination, was a clip, one of many that a top LTTE operative had brought in from Jaffna. It showed female LTTE cadres somewhere in the north of the island nation marching to the tune of a martial band. To the SIT, the flag-bearer at the head of the group bore a remarkable resemblance to Dhanu.

In August 1991, *The Hindu's Frontline* magazine ran a story that corroborated the SIT's conclusions on Dhanu's antecedents as a child of the cause for Tamil Eelam. It said she was the daughter of Rajaratnam, a Sri Lankan Tamil nationalist who had inspired Prabhakaran when the former signed on as one of the earliest members of the Ilankai Thamil Arasu Katchi, and the Puli Padai, the Tiger Army.

In June of that year, only days after the assassination, and in a departure from normal practice, Prabhakaran honoured his hero Rajaratnam and others, including the Tamil Nadu-based Kasi Anandan, in a special ceremony, even though the former had been dead for sixteen long years, while in exile in Madras. Was this a disguised tribute to Dhanu? The only way that Prabhakaran could say thank you, perhaps?

The LTTE quickly got into the act, using a resident of Urumpirai in Jaffna to put out an elaborate denial of Dhanu's parentage. Any confirmation that she was a serving member of the LTTE would expose their role in the assassination—and they did not want that made public. After all, this was a terror group that dreamed of a Greater Eelam and being known as the killers of Rajiv Gandhi, who was adored by Tamilians, would mean losing support in Tamil Nadu.

Claiming that Dhanu had no link to the Rajaratnam family, the Urumpirai resident added that Rajaratnam's second wife and their second daughter, Anuja, were in fact in mourning, as the youngest daughter, Kalaivani aka Capt. Akino, had died in battle, while Anuja herself was recovering from injuries in another skirmish with the Sri Lankan army. Rajaratnam's eldest daughter, Vasugi, and a son, Sivavarman, from his first marriage, the man said, lived in Canada.

Despite the lie, SIT's skilful skull superimposition conclusively proved that Dhanu was the same girl as the one named Capt. Akino, codenamed Anbu, who was heading the march.

This would make her Rajaratnam's daughter—real name Kalaivani aka Gayatri aka Thenmozhi Rajaratnam, resident of Kaithadi, Nunavil, Chavakacheri, born on 26 July 1968, purportedly died 8 September 1991, according to the LTTE's diary of heroes, *Maaverar Kuripedu*.

The interpolation of Dhanu's real name into the list of the 243 young women who died in battle in September 1991 wasn't too difficult, the SIT investigators concluded.

Given the sustained propaganda against the IPKF, the prevailing view among the Sri Lankan Tamils was that

Dhanu had been willing to give up her life to avenge the many alleged rapes and violations of Lankan Tamil women by the Indian soldiers, including, allegedly, a close relative and, some say, even herself.

Norwegian peace negotiators like Erik Solheim say, 'She may have been barely sixteen at the time the IPKF were deployed in Jaffna, and the prevailing story, every time the subject was brought up was that either she or a member of her family had been raped. And, that this was payback.'

The bomb itself was put together piece by piece, with the 9-volt batteries and the various switches, toggles and wires, and the 0.2-mm diameter metallic balls and pellets. These were bought by Kumaran Pathmanathan or 'KP', chief arms procurer for the LTTE, from arms merchants across the world, and put together locally by Perarivalan, the Indian LTTE sympathizer, along with Murugan. The actual IED and the pellets and grenades were probably brought in through the worldwide network of smugglers that KP oversaw, who had easy access to India's coastline.

The deputy head of the Black Tigresses, Akila, had described Dhanu—barely twenty-three when she blew herself to bits—as a 'child of fire', a veiled reference to the human bomb.

But what is really interesting is that the SIT's remarkable information gatherers give 'credit' for the human-bomb concept, not to Prabhakaran as everyone else universally did—and does—but to the deputy head of the Karampuli, the Black Tigress, Akila, who came up with the idea of strapping an IED on a person's body to gain access to the target—in this case, Rajiv Gandhi—long before it was adopted by the Taliban and the Islamists in the Arab world as their weapon of choice.

Lt Col. Akila, who would die in battle in October 1995, was the SIT's Accused No. 3. Only Prabhakaran and Pottu Amman, being Accused No. 1 and Accused No. 2 respectively, were higher on the list.

~

When the Walls Close In

As the photographs of the assassins of Rajiv Gandhi were splashed across the city of Madras and Tamil Nadu and the neighbouring states through early June, Sivaresan, forced to go into hiding, continued to use his secret wireless radio to communicate with LTTE intelligence chief Pottu Amman in Jaffna, updating him on the arrests of members of the hit squad and various LTTE supporters, pushing all the while for a safe passage home for himself and the fallback suicide bomber, Subha.

When a reward was announced for anyone who had information about them—Rs 10 lakh for Sivaresan and Rs 5 lakh for Subha—the SIT was besieged with tip-offs.

But Pottu Amman had no intention of letting these two key operatives fall into the hands of the SIT and, in message after message, asked them to lie low and ensure they had their cyanide pills with them at all times, a signal that they must evade capture at any cost.

With President's rule in place in Tamil Nadu post the assassination, and a heightened security alert, the LTTE's smuggling of arms and people between the coasts had virtually ended. Every boat, every smuggler, every gun-runner was being watched and monitored.

Sivaresan's access to his own Tiger network inside Tamil Nadu was severely curtailed when the SIT began picking up both Lankan and Indian Tamil LTTE supporters across the state.

In Dindigul, the police stumbled upon what would be the LTTE's fifth column inside Tamil Nadu, the so-called Tamil National Retrieval Troops and the Tamizhar Pasarai, headed by a pro-LTTE Indian Tamil, Ravichandran, who had been sending Tamil youths to be trained in Jaffna. He had been tasked by the LTTE supremo with destabilizing the southern state on the lines of Jammu and Kashmir as part of the quest to create a Greater Eelam that spanned the Palk Strait.

Prabhakaran believed—mistakenly—that once Rajiv Gandhi had been eliminated, the Tamils, with the active support of the local Indian political parties, would rise up to fight the Indian state alongside the LTTE and the country would plunge into chaos and disintegrate.

Pottu Amman, realizing that the walls were closing in on his man, activated his well-entrenched intelligence chief in Tamil Nadu, Tiruchy Santhan, and his aide, Irumborai, to arrange for the escape of the three people in the know of the assassination—Sivaresan, Subha and the wireless operator named Nehru—rather than let them fall into the hands of investigators and conclusively implicate the LTTE.

But the boat sent by Pottu Amman sank before it made landfall.

SIT sleuths, who recall the hunt for the assassins, recount how Sivaresan simply dropped off the face of the earth for nearly three weeks, even though he was now relying exclusively on the LTTE intelligence network run by Tiruchy Santhan that RAW and IB operatives had always closely tracked.

In fact, it was being tracked even more closely, now that they had proof that the Prabhakaran protégé was being shepherded from one location to the next by Tiruchy Santhan's wireless operator, a man named Dixon, and the LTTE's intelligence group operative named Kanthan. In a bid to rattle the LTTE and let them know they were on to them, even though in reality they had no idea where Sivaresan really was, the SIT published the two men's pictures.

The SIT finally closed in on Dixon after two of his associates were caught and one of them, Vicky, spilled the beans about Dixon's Coimbatore lair. It was the centre, they discovered, for a clandestine LTTE-managed factory to manufacture grenade shells. As the SIT closed in, Dixon took his own life on 28 July and, critically, destroyed the wireless set that Tiruchy Santhan had been using to contact Pottu Amman. By then, Kanthan had escaped to Jaffna.

Dixon's associate Vicky also told them about the man who had been entrusted by Tiruchy Santhan to take care of Sivaresan—Suresh Master—and the two cars, a green Maruti and a blue air-conditioned Premier Padmini, that were being used by the group to get around the state from one safe house to another.

Sometime in late July or early August, Suresh Master, working with his LTTE colleague Rangan, pulled off Sivaresan and Subha's escape from Madras in a move that was nothing short of masterly. Rangan approached a Mettur transporter and LTTE sympathizer, Dhanasekharan aka Raja, to give them an empty oil tanker, into which he smuggled Sivaresan, Subha and Nehru, and escorted them, through the night of 2 August (one version claims it could have been as early as 28 July) through the neighbouring state of Karnataka and into Bangalore, without once being stopped or arousing the suspicion of the police!

Bangalore is where everything that could go wrong, did. But it would be another sixteen days before the SIT would finally track them down to their new lair.

Suresh Master had managed, unknown to the Bangalore city police and intelligence officials, to shelter and treat dozens of his injured colleagues from the LTTE in two safe houses in the city—one in Indiranagar, the other in Domlur. He had used a Bangalore-based lathe operator, Ranganath, to find these safe houses, including one for Sivaresan and Subha, without telling him who it was for. Ranganath first took the group to his own home, a house in Puttenahalli that he had rented for himself from a Congress partyman, Anjaneya.

In the charged atmosphere, the SIT was picking up one LTTE operative after another, each one a mine of information, lifting the lid off the incredible network of support that the Tigers had set up over the years. But Ranganath was a new addition to the ranks, and his movements and modus operandi were therefore that much more difficult to track, a senior police official told me.

Vicky's revelations would finally lead to Sivaresan. His tip-off on a safe house in Tippasandra, Indiranagar, that was used by Tiruchy Santhan, was expected to yield Sivaresan. Instead, when the police stormed this LTTE hideout on 5 August, they found two injured LTTE boys, both of whom bit into their cyanide capsules. One died instantly; the other, three days later.

The SIT then tapped a Bangalore-based LTTE sympathizer named Jagannathan, who squealed about the handful of other hideouts in the city—each one a revelation to the police—which led them to a single-storeyed house on a quiet side street in Domlur, which abuts Indiranagar.

When the SIT and the Black Cats raided the Domlur house—now on 14th Main, HAL second stage—after locals caught and thrashed one of the LTTE injured, mistaking him for a thief as he was coming home, they realized how close they had been to nabbing Rajiv Gandhi's assassins. Sivaresan, Subha and Nehru, the senior police official discovered, 'had been at the Domlur house overnight and must have been there when we stormed the other Indiranagar hideout in Tippasandra'.

In fact, when the LTTE hit squad came to their first hideout, waiting to receive them was the burly Tiruchy Santhan himself! (In a botched attempt, the SIT was unable to nab Tiruchy Santhan alive. He was running out of places to hide when they finally cornered him several months later in November 1991 in an LTTE smuggler's house in Tiruchy, where he consumed cyanide and died.)

Uncomfortable and uneasy about Puttenahalli, where they stood out from the local Kannadigas, Sivaresan had moved to Domlur, even as Ranganath found a house in Muthati and another in Biroota in Mandya district for the other injured cadres under Suresh Master's care. The new hideout for the nervous and edgy Sivaresan was a single-storeyed house in Konanakunte, some 20 kilometres away, on the outskirts of the city.

Ranganath, who had had both the cars re-painted and their number plates changed, was given little choice but to move to Konanakunte with the group, given that he now knew they were all complicit in Rajiv Gandhi's assassination. He was now a co-conspirator.

Ranganath's wife, Mridula, uneasy, angry and afraid after she discovered the identities of her husband's new friends, accompanied them when they moved to the remote colony on the outskirts of Bangalore on 16 August. Suresh Master was taking no chances, even though Ranganath had grown sympathetic to the Tiger cause and was no longer doing it just for the money.

Moving to Konanakunte was a fatal error of judgement for the Rajiv Gandhi hit squad. Cornered and hunted, moving from one safe house to another, denied a seaborne escape route, and in completely unfamiliar territory, Sivaresan probably sensed that they were running out of options.

For the SIT and the city police, unschooled in storming hideouts, capturing Sivaresan and the other members of the hit squad alive would prove a challenge unless they were backed up by the Black Cat commandos. Before that happened, they had to find the elusive Tiger.

Two things would lead the police to Sivaresan's doorstep before the SIT. One, Ranganath's contact numbers and home address were collected by police when they were checking to see who had rented the Muthati and Biroota houses. It led them to a Congress worker, Anjaneya, as the main contact in Puttenahalli, who gave Ranganath's office address as the lathe factory in Mandya, and his home address as Puttenahalli alongside the Shanti Oliver church, where Ranganath's brother-in-law was a pastor. It wouldn't take long for the city police to trace him. Two, the newspapers that Ranganath brought back with him to the house when he went to buy milk that morning had front-paged the Muthati raid and the LTTE suicides, deeply upsetting both Sivaresan and Suresh Master, who reportedly muttered that they were being chased and hunted like dogs. It clearly threw them off their game.

But the person most rattled by the news that Rajiv Gandhi's assassins were in the state—and now in her own home and backyard—was Mridula. Claiming to be ill and suffering an asthmatic attack, Mridula simply upped and left. Strangely, not one of the hardcore and well-armed LTTE operatives, neither Suresh Master nor Sivaresan, as much as protested. She left with Ranganath, but on their way home to Puttenahalli, he got off and decided to head back to Konanakunte to his new friends. The doughty and deeply patriotic Mridula, outraged by the assassination of Rajiv Gandhi, knew she had to do the right thing. She called the police and blew the whistle on the entire clandestine operation, describing in detail to the shocked, unsuspecting police, the sixteen days she had spent with Rajiv Gandhi's assassins, and how the most wanted men in India were now holed up in a house, barely 20 kilometres outside the city, poised, armed for a counter-attack.

Bangalore City Police took her away to be debriefed, but then made the monumental error of sending uniformed and armed men to Konanakunte. They compounded that error by surrounding the suspects' house with police vehicles that were clearly visible from the hideout.

Ranganath, who had spent the night holed up in a 'lodge', returned to Puttenahalli early on the morning of 19 August to check on his wife and was told that she had been taken away by police. Panicking, he made tracks for Konanakunte, arriving in an autorickshaw. It didn't help matters when he was recognized by the local residents, particularly the milk vendor, who thrashed him soundly for sheltering Rajiv Gandhi's assassins and handed him over to the police.

By this time, hundreds of curious local residents had gathered around the Konanakunte house, as had the city police, who had been led there by whistle-blower Mridula. This is where Sivaresan, Subha and Nehru, along with Suresh Master and two others, would make their last stand.

The SIT's own debriefing of Mridula only happened late on Sunday, 18 August, after the police commissioner informed them of the tip-off.

With only a few Black Cats on call and the NSG put on operational alert, the SIT knew that by the time they got to the spot, they would have lost the all-too-important element of surprise.

The lack of camaraderie and co-operation between the local police and the SIT, unlike the close relationship enjoyed by the SIT and Tamil Nadu Police, was partly to blame for the delayed alert, and it would yield the expected consequences.

Mridula's information and her graphic description of the lightly armed LTTE team left the SIT with a small sense of satisfaction as they believed that their hard work was about to pay off, and they would finally get their hands on the men and the woman who had pulled off the sensational and shocking murder of a national icon. Alive or dead.

At first toying with the idea of sending Mridula or the milk vendor into the house as a decoy, the SIT tracking team discarded the proposal as being too tricky. They knew that the only chance they had of getting Sivaresan and Subha alive was to ensure they did not access the cyanide capsules they carried on their person or turn their grenades and guns on themselves.

For the assassins, time was running out. There was nowhere to run or hide. For both the hunters and the hunted, the next few hours would prove to be critical.

~

It was 17 August 1991. If he had survived, Rajiv Gandhi would have been celebrating his forty-seventh birthday in three days. It was also three months, almost to the day, since Sivaresan had assassinated him.

Deputy Commissioner of Police K. Seetharam, who looked after Rajiv Gandhi's security detail when he was prime minister, had chosen to come back to Karnataka in 1990. He had been devastated by the death of his favourite politician, particularly by the manner in which he had been cut down in his prime.

At the time, sandalwood smuggler Veerappan consumed most of his attention. So, when he was summoned late on the night of 17 August to move to Muthati village near Mandya, and from there to Biroota, where locals had reported suspicious activity, the last thing he expected was to stumble upon LTTE operatives.

By the time Seetharam and his team arrived early the next morning, at 2 a.m., and raided the hideouts, of the nine who had been hiding out in Muthati and the eight in Biroota, twelve had already died after consuming cyanide. Three would die later. Two had survived and were taken to Bowring hospital in Bangalore for treatment.

Seetharam says that with the stepped-up hunt for Rajiv Gandhi's killers, he could never understand why he or, for that matter, any SIT member or top cop was not given access to these survivors and allowed to interrogate them, however junior or inconsequential or near death, they may have been.

'It didn't make any sense,' he said. 'The entire country was fixated on Rajiv Gandhi's killers and nobody thought it necessary to question the two survivors.'

The next night, around 11 p.m., there was another summons from his top bosses at the police headquarters. This time, they were told that they had been tipped off about an entire team of LTTE operatives, which included Rajiv Gandhi's killers, hiding out in Konanakunte. He and his colleague Prabhakar, and a handful of commandos from the NSG, rushed to the suburb and surrounded the house in the dead of night. Their team kept watch from the only other building in the vicinity, the house next door.

The hideout itself was in complete darkness. It showed absolutely no activity. All the windows were shut. Nobody could see them from the house; they couldn't see anything in the house either.

Suresh's man Rangan, however, while returning from the village, spotted the police vehicles that were surrounding the residence and the uniformed, armed men taking their positions, and made good his escape in the Maruti. He would be nabbed several days later when he arrived in Madras and foolishly went straight back to his place of work.

With Rangan's failure to return, and Ranganath and Mridula having left the hideout, the Tigers at Konanakunte quickly realized that they had no access to a car or, for that matter, a driver. Escape by road was therefore impossible. They didn't know the local language, Kannada, and were stranded in a place they knew little or nothing about; they had no maps, no access to fresh food and water. In remote Konanakunte, they had no local support as they would have had if they had stayed on in Tamil Nadu.

Seetharam believes the police, for the first time since Indiranagar, Muthati and Biroota, had the tiniest of advantages but, for some reason, their hand was stayed and they were told to simply stay put until reinforcements—with cyanide antidotes arrived.

'The problem was, anyone looking at us from that house could see us and our people in the stairwell, and, as the sun came up, there we were, fully armed with Sten guns, barely 50 yards from the front door. We had lost the element of surprise. We should have stormed in immediately and captured Sivaresan and Subha alive. But despite repeated requests to our bosses, we were told to sit it out and wait for further orders. That the SIT, the Black Cat commandos were on their way, that the chief was coming, that Muthati had gone wrong because we had rushed in, we should wait for the cyanide antidote . . .

'We were the field unit on the ground, we should have been consulted, our views taken on board. We should have stormed the house on the night of 18 August. I have no idea what we were waiting for,' he said, showing me pictures of himself and his family with Rajiv Gandhi in happier times. He believes that the delay was because the top brass wanted to be there and corner all the glory—and the awards—when the commandos stormed the house.

With his frustration coming through even twenty-five years after the event, Seetharam recounts how, on the morning of 19 August, members of the press arrived at their doorstep, as did the only television channels at the time, Doordarshan and Star News. If they weren't visible before, there was no missing them now!

'We just sat around and did absolutely nothing from 4 a.m. till sundown,' he says.

At 6.15 p.m., he says there was a flash of light from inside the house. Some fifteen minutes later, one man emerged into the portico and began shouting loudly as he fired several rounds from a machine gun before going back inside.

'Bullets were ricocheting all over the place as we scrambled for cover, with one bullet missing me narrowly,' recalls the top cop. 'The shooter was aiming, for some strange reason, at the only other building that existed in that area, and a lorry that was parked to the left of the hideout.'

Seetharam recalls that after the man went inside, there was a burst of fire from the back of the house—probably the shooter and another man making an attempt to see if the party could escape from there—before there was a blast from inside the house, and then it all fell eerily silent again.

Even then, the police officers weren't allowed to enter the hideout. Their instructions were that they should wait until the commando team and top cops Kaarthikeyan and the local police biggie Kempaiah, the additional director general of police, Crime—and currently adviser to Karnataka Chief Minister Siddaramaiah—arrived.

At 6 a.m. the following morning, when the hideout was finally stormed by the Black Cats who had landed with the top brass only forty-five minutes earlier, they found that Sivaresan had been shot in the temple, while Subha, Nehru and Suresh Master, and three others with them, had bitten on the cyanide capsules and died, bleeding from their mouths and ears, their faces contorted in agony, their bodies twisted in pain.

This was it, the final denouement . . . This was no blaze of glory, no roaring Tiger fighting and dying for a cause, but craven and cowardly, the Tigers and their Karampuli, the fallback Black Tigress, collapsing in a whimper.

Either by accident or design, it was Rajiv Gandhi's birthday.

3

The Jaffna Conspiracy

IN THE DENSE JUNGLES OF north-eastern Sri Lanka, across the Palk Strait, Prabhakaran nursed a grudge against Rajiv Gandhi which would become a full-scale obsession. It was here, deep in the forests of the Wanni, that the plot to kill the former Indian prime minister was first hatched.

As the LTTE chief, solitary and furtive, moved like a hunted animal under the cover of darkness from one hideout to another, night after night, from Jaffna and Kankesanthurai to Vadamarachchi, and Vavuniya and back, the depth of his fury at Rajiv Gandhi's perceived perfidy was an open secret. That is, it was a secret to everyone but the Indians.

Through the IPKF deployment in the north-east, he played a game of cat and mouse with Delhi. Knowing he would be easy prey if he broke cover, he rarely slept in the same bed twice, neither took nor made any telephone calls, trusting no one, staying one step ahead of both

Colombo and Delhi. It was a habit that stayed with him till his last days.

His only entertainment after he was forced to return to the island nation from India in 1987 came from a movie projector in the safe house he picked to hide out for the night. This is where he would watch the latest thriller play out as shadows on a blank wall. The Tiger chief's obsessive paranoia fed off Kollywood, the Tamil movies that featured his idol, MGR, in the lead, and films of the same genre as the 1984 Kamal Haasan-starrer *Oru Kaidhiyin Diary* (A Convict's Diary) that spun stories of angry men nursing a grievance, extracting retribution, driven by revenge.

A school dropout, Prabhakaran did have his Achilles' heel. It wasn't wine or women or song, or books—he grew up on Phantom comics—it was the movies. He was addicted to the string of videos brought to him by the one RAW agent with whom he shared a very special rapport— the legendary S. Chandrasekharan, known affectionately by the moniker 'Chandran'.

Chandrasekharan, who retired from RAW and set up the respected Delhi-based think tank, the South Asia Analysis Group, says it was from these nightly thrillers that the Jaffna conspiracy to assassinate Rajiv Gandhi probably took its inspiration. The Fred Zinnemann 1973 movie, *The Day of the Jackal*, based on the Frederick Forsyth bestseller, was the probable first seed.

Prabhakaran routinely settled scores by publicly eliminating his rivals to instil fear in his enemies; his first 'kill' was the Jaffna mayor Alfred Duraiappah in 1975, whom he reportedly shot as he entered the Varadaraja Perumal temple. Chandran believes the plan to assassinate Rajiv Gandhi was in keeping with this 'kill or get killed' philosophy. 'Everyone thinks it was the CIA and Mossad that planted the idea of assassinating Rajiv Gandhi in Prabhakaran's head. I believe it was the movies that he saw; that's what gave him the idea,' says Chandran. Conspiracy theorists, however, demur.

It wasn't that Delhi didn't have him within sight. If Prabhakaran wanted to get back at India for trying to call the shots in his backyard, India had mobilized every resource at its command to have eyes on their prize target at all times.

But as a RAW operative from that era freely admits, with surveillance dependant on tip-offs from Lankan Tamils outside the inner circle, they never knew precisely where he was at any given moment. 'We knew the minute he left that location,' he laughs. Close, but never close enough.

Delhi undoubtedly had ample opportunity to eliminate the LTTE chief a number of times—and chose not to. As a senior member of the Indian Air Force (IAF), who served in the IPKF and was stationed as the IAF bases in Palaly and Trincomalee, recounts, he and the helicopter squadron he commanded had been given Prabhakaran's co-ordinates.

'I had my copter, all ready to go. We informed headquarters that we had been tipped off on where he was. One of our chaps had tracked him down. It was all systems go. All we needed was clearance from Delhi and we could eliminate him. Just like that,' he says, snapping his fingers. 'We waited for the signal but then came the message—a firm "no"', says the senior Air Force pilot. 'We had him in our sights. If we had eliminated him then, who knows ...' he says with a shrug, leaving the sentence hanging.

Only once thereafter did the IPKF get close enough to Prabhakaran. They bombed his bunker in the Wanni, in his hideout Base One Four, in January 1989. The LTTE chief, though angry and upset, escaped with barely a scratch.

Complicating matters was the confusion and lack of clarity in Delhi's intelligence and strategic circles, on whether Prabhakaran constituted a short-term threat to be eliminated or a long-term asset to be cultivated. And added to this was the question of whether this bit player who had forcefully interjected himself into the Indo-Sri Lanka narrative by taking on the Indian Army, could still be 'turned'; a Tamil 'card' that India could use to keep Colombo off balance in the years to come.

Prabhakaran was under no illusions about where he stood vis-à-vis Delhi. He may have made concessions on a one-on-one basis to Indians like Chandran, but Rajiv Gandhi's Delhi was the enemy.

In fact, the RAW operative's relationship with the LTTE chief and the man that RAW cultivated as its LTTE insider, Col Kittu, real name Sathasivan Krishnakumar, was so strong that when Indian soldiers were being held prisoner by the LTTE, it was Chandran—as he himself admits—whom the Indian Army called for help.

'They asked me to intercede with the LTTE and get our men released,' he says. 'I did. I stepped in when Military Intelligence [MI] asked for help.' He knew the Lankan Tamil leaders like few others, all were on a first-name basis with him.

Chandran was low-key, nondescript. RAW recruits of that time still recall how, in the mid-1980s, he would simply throw a bag over his shoulder, get on a motorbike and zoom off from their office in Madras and not be seen or heard of for months together. Their guess was that Chandran, the only Indian who could reach out to the top rungs of the Tamil militant groups, had either headed off to Jaffna on a clandestine boat or to one of the many camps in the state where the Tamil groups were being given military training.

Thirty years later, incidentally, Chandran continues to staunchly deny that Indian operatives trained the Lankan Tamil separatists. 'We didn't need to. One group of Tamils had already travelled to Palestine and received military training from George Habash's wing of the PLO [Palestine Liberation Organization]. When that first group came back, they trained the others; India had no role to play in giving them military training,' insists Chandran, as politically correct as ever, leaving out the fact that India had provided refuge and set up the camps where the Tamils trained.

Thirty years later, as difficult as it is for him to accept, Chandran also acknowledges that Prabhakaran's black warrant for Rajiv Gandhi was unexpected.

'I didn't see it coming. I thought I knew him, but one didn't expect this. It makes me want to weep; it saddens me deeply that we were unable to save Rajiv Gandhi. We should have saved him, we should have known. We didn't really get Prabhakaran,' says Chandran.

Many members of his RAW fraternity as well as senior members of India's military who served in Sri Lanka with the IPKF have gone public over the years with their disquiet on the role played by the Colombo elite and the political families, particularly President Premadasa who is said to have fuelled Prabhakaran's antipathy towards Rajiv Gandhi. Rajiv Gandhi was a leader whom Colombo and, for that matter, Pakistan's counter-intelligence agency, Inter-Services Intelligence (ISI), which had a major presence in the Sri Lankan capital, did not want to see return to lead India.

And Prabhakaran was easy pickings for anyone wanting to settle scores with 'Big Brother'. India paid him scant attention to begin with, preferring Lankan Tamil groups such as the People's Liberation Organisation of Tamil Eelam (PLOTE) and EPRLF.

As India played footsie with the other groups, the LTTE grew more powerful, tightening its hold over the Tamil people under an ever more menacing Prabhakaran who refused to be relegated to the margins of the Tamil discourse. Delhi could no longer afford to ignore him. But in trying to contain and manage him, they erred, and erred badly.

Prabhakaran first came to Chandran's notice after his active role in the butchery of eleven Sri Lankan soldiers, the incident that triggered the July 1983 race riots in Colombo, and the storming of the Anuradhapura temple that killed more than 140 worshippers and monks two years later. That, and the earlier shootout on PLOTE leader Uma Maheswaran in Madras in broad daylight in 1982, after the two had fallen out, when Prabhakaran was detained but jumped bail, had RAW's instant attention.

From then on, Prabhakaran, who had launched his own violent, separatist movement with barely fifty men to call his own, was on Chandran's radar. Chandran was one of the few who felt they understood and empathized with the angry young man from Velvettithurai—and the others drawn to him—who took up arms against Colombo.

A man of few words, Prabhakaran, who took refuge in India in 1983 and received arms training in a camp on the

Tamil Nadu–Karnataka border, met Rajiv Gandhi for the first time at 10, Janpath in June 1985, after he was picked out from the crowd for his leadership potential.

'He spoke little, but he would hear you out, let you say whatever you wanted to say, never sharing what he really thought. The only time you knew what he was thinking was when he got angry. For Prabhakaran, the one thing he could never forgive was treachery. He would fly into a rage, get completely incensed about it and pronounce a death sentence,' says Chandran, describing the mindset of the LTTE chief.

It was Chandran and his team who reportedly shepherded Prabhakaran to pivotal meetings with Rajiv Gandhi, particularly the last one on 29 July 1987, when the LTTE leader was forced to accept—albeit only verbally—that he supported a unitary Sri Lanka. This was hours before the Indian premier headed to Sri Lanka where he would ink the Indo-Sri Lanka peace accord with Sri Lankan President Junius Jayewardene, thereby ending Prabhakaran's dreams for a separate nation.

Those present at that meeting at 10, Janpath that day—including LTTE ideologue Anton Balasingham—would later remark on how sanguine Prabhakaran seemed at the time. Did he mistakenly believe that he did not have to support the accord in public and would have to do no more than make a token surrender of arms, or was he simply masking his anger, biding his time until he could take revenge?

He was gifted a bulletproof jacket that Rajiv Gandhi owned; it was placed on Prabhakaran's shoulders by Rajiv Gandhi's young son, Rahul, with Rajiv Gandhi saying, 'Take care of yourself.' Rajiv Gandhi's naivety? Perhaps.

Officials at the July meeting, including the then foreign minister, P.V. Narasimha Rao, told Rajiv Gandhi that Prabhakaran could not be trusted, and the Congress leader reportedly dismissed them saying, 'Prabhakaran has given his word. I trust him.'

The LTTE leader had shown little emotion. Where once he had bristled at being treated like a bit player, no more than a sideshow in the run-up to the July 1985 peace talks in Thimpu and to the November 1986 SAARC summit in Bangalore, now, he kept his cool. He had taken the slights in his stride in the past, believing it was worth his while as long as India supported the LTTE's quest for Eelam, as it had the creation of Bangladesh. Had the worm turned? Or had he seen the writing on the wall and deliberately kept his counsel?

When he was escorted back to Ashok Hotel after meeting Rajiv Gandhi in 1987, the real Prabhakaran opened up, ranting and raving in Tamil to his 'friend' Vaiko, the Tamil Nadu politician V. Gopalaswamy, with whom he had built a bond, saying that he had been 'betrayed'. He repeated much the same thought when he was forcibly flown back to Jaffna in August and spoke to the press there soon after.

Once the Tigers were forced to actually de-weaponize and the EPRLF were primed to take charge of the north and the east in elections to the council held under the purview of the IPKF, Prabhakaran fully understood his newly diminished status. That became the genesis for his grudge against his newfound nemesis, Rajiv Gandhi.

As journalist and author M.R. Narayan Swamy correctly surmised in his book *The Tiger Vanquished*,[1] Prabhakaran may not have played by the rules himself, jettisoning fair play when it suited him. But betray him, and vengeance and death were certain.

In October 1989, as the IPKF began reducing its military footprint under pressure from the Sri Lankan government and the LTTE's guerrilla tactics, Prabhakaran was putting the finishing touches to his 'hate' list. Leaders of the other Lankan Tamil political groups who competed with him for the fealty of the Tamil people were on it. But topping the list was the Indian prime minister who had robbed him of his dream of heading a separate Tamil state.

In April 1990, as the last of the IPKF forces began to withdraw from Sri Lanka after a thirty-two-month deployment, Prabhakaran emerged from his jungle hideout, where he had remained hidden for over two and

---

[1] M.R. Narayan Swamy, *The Tiger Vanquished* (New Delhi: Sage Publications, 2010).

a half years, and met the press. In response to a question by a Sri Lankan journalist from the *Sunday Times* on why he had turned against Rajiv Gandhi and the IPKF, Prabhakaran, who rarely shared his innermost thoughts, had this to say: 'The LTTE are not against the Indian people or the Indian government but they are against the former administrator of India.' In other words, Rajiv Gandhi. Tragically, neither the IB nor RAW picked up on that first warning shot.

In the first week of May 1990, on a sweltering day, deep in the jungles beyond Jaffna, long before anyone had an inkling of what he intended, Prabhakaran began to move the pawns on his 'Kill Rajiv Gandhi' chessboard. He summoned his intelligence chief, Pottu Amman, and, for the first time, voiced the idea of eliminating Rajiv Gandhi. Both Pottu Amman and one of Prabhakaran's trusted bodyguards who was present, strongly advised him against it, an LTTE sympathizer who was close to the developments told me.

'They warned him that the consequences of eliminating the leader of another country as powerful as India would be grave,' the sympathizer said.

Pottu Amman knew it would rob the LTTE of its only safe haven across the Palk Strait where he sent his wounded cadres for treatment, and alienate the Indian Tamils who supported and backed their cause. The other complication was that the Indian Army now knew the lay of the land better than when they had first arrived in August 1987 and would be a much more difficult force to tackle.

Prabhakaran is said to have agreed with them. But what he didn't tell them was that he had not given up on the idea. Instead, he began to put his Plan B into action. To his LTTE commanders, it would be sold as a plan to get rid of Padmanabha of the EPRLF, a man whose rise would have eclipsed the Tigers. For Prabhakaran, it would be a trial run for a possible Rajiv Gandhi assassination.

In running the IPKF out of town in 1990, Prabhakaran believed he had cleared the LTTE's own path to power. But within a month of the IPKF's exit, Sri Lankan President Premadasa had begun negotiations with the EPRLF to put a friendlier, more amenable Tamil government in place in the north and the east. The LTTE had come in useful to rid the island of Indian forces. But that's where it ended. Premadasa no longer had any use for the LTTE.

Prabhakaran would settle scores with Premadasa later, having him assassinated by a Tamil suicide bomber in May 1993, an official investigation by Colombo's deputy inspector general of the Criminal Investigation Department, Amarasena Rajapakse, would later show. The LTTE leader's mole, a bisexual valet he had planted in the President's household who became his eyes and ears, tipped the Tigers off about the election meeting where Premadasa would be blown up, Rajiv Gandhi-style, by a suicide bomber. The LTTE chief was incensed by Sri Lankan officialdom's active co-operation with Indian officers investigating Rajiv Gandhi's assassination when they arrived in Colombo in June 1991, which helped identify all the main players involved, and would conclusively implicate Prabhakaran.

Ragothaman, part of the SIT, says that Premadasa's role in Rajiv Gandhi's assassination has never been fully explored; as does Lt Gen. A.S. Kalkat, the general officer commanding-in-chief of the IPKF.

But in early June 1990, Prabhakaran had other things on his mind. He summoned Pottu Amman again. He asked him to find a man who could travel to Tamil Nadu and eliminate Padmanabha. Two weeks later, Padmanabha, along with thirteen others, was murdered in an LTTE-style elimination operation on 19 June 1990 at the EPRLF office in Madras by a crack LTTE team hand-picked by Prabhakaran. Heading the team was Sivaresan, the man named 'One-eyed Jack' by the Indian media, who would pull off the assassination of Rajiv Gandhi eleven months later, a stone's throw away from the same city, using the same kind of bomb-making materials.

The Padmanabha hit was more than a dry run for the Rajiv Gandhi assassination. Prabhakaran had found his assassin.

In August 1990, an early copy of an interview that Rajiv Gandhi had given to the ABP publication *Sunday* to mark his birthday, reinforced Prabhakaran's resolve to eliminate him. This time, neither Pottu Amman nor the other members of his inner circle, like Akila—who trained the two girls picked to be suicide bombers—could disagree.

The *Sunday* interview had Rajiv Gandhi spelling out his Sri Lanka policy in no uncertain terms: 'Today, they are saying "we will never send Indian troops anywhere" or something like that . . . If a friendly country needs help, what will we do? Maldives asked for help. Were we supposed to say no and let the United States send people to the Maldives? This government would be totally abrogating its responsibility to the region . . . creating a vacuum that others will fill.'

In the same interview Rajiv Gandhi also said, 'The IPKF was in Sri Lanka to fight for the unity and integrity of Sri Lanka.'

Prabhakaran wanted a separate state. Rajiv Gandhi, who had no illusions about India's growing status as a responsible South Asian power, stood between him and his dream.

Despite losing the November 1989 polls and declining to head a minority government, Rajiv Gandhi's Congress still had the largest number of MPs in the Lok Sabha, which made him powerful enough to pull down governments if he wanted to—and, to a great extent, influence policy. And now, much to the chagrin of the Tigers, a year later, he was on the comeback trail.

By September 1990, Prabhakaran had set the Rajiv Gandhi assassination plan in motion by quietly dispatching the first set of conspirators—a man named Vijayan; his wife, Selvi; and her father, Bhaskaran—all posing as refugees, to India. Their house in Kodungaiyur, Madras, would be the first of many safe houses that the assassination squads would use, as the SIT investigation into the 21 May murderous attack would find.

As V.P. Singh's National Front government looked ever more shaky, Prabhakaran, in early October 1990, summoned his key advisers for a crucial meeting to assess the chances of the Congress president returning to power. The consensus was that a Rajiv Gandhi comeback was all but certain, which meant two things to the LTTE leader—Indian forces would be re-deployed in north-east Sri Lanka to enforce Rajiv Gandhi's pet project, and the deep-rooted LTTE network set up in Tamil Nadu with the active co-operation of the DK and the DMK would be dismantled.

This time, the canny Prabhakaran was able to bring his military commanders round to his view that assassinating Rajiv Gandhi was the only option to safeguard the LTTE's interests. But only his inner circle would be privy to this.

By November 1990, the V.P. Singh government did fall and the former fiery 'Young Turk' Chandrashekhar became caretaker prime minister, his government supported from the outside by Rajiv Gandhi's Congress party. To

Prabhakaran, this wasn't the best news. A mid-term poll seemed like a very real possibility and in the event of Rajiv Gandhi becoming prime minister, his SPG-provided security would be virtually impenetrable.

The only way he could be eliminated was if they struck when he was still in the Opposition, or when he was on the campaign trail where security would be noticeably lax. The irony is that the plot unfolded right under the nose of the IB. Although it had established the nexus between the DK, the DMK and the LTTE, and based on that, had the DMK government in Tamil Nadu led by the pro-LTTE Karunanidhi dismissed, they failed to connect the dots or prevent the LTTE from continuing to operate as freely as it did before President's rule was imposed in the state.

By the end of November, Prabhakaran's plan was all but ready. He summoned his Madras-based LTTE propaganda chief 'Baby' Subramaniam to Jaffna, who arrived in the LTTE headquarters in the first week of December and was the first man outside the inner circle to be briefed on the Tiger chief's high-profile target.

Prabhakaran was confident of Pottu Amman's protégé Sivaresan's ability to pull off the hit. Sivaresan was to be assisted by two people—Muthuraja and Murugan; the first, the LTTE's 'go-to' man in Madras, and the second, a Jaffna-based explosives expert.

By the beginning of 1991, Prabhakaran's chosen quartet was at work. 'Baby' Subramaniam and Muthuraja began to widen the circle of their LTTE network in Madras, looking for families that could provide a cover for the gang of assassins that was being readied to cross the Palk Strait.

They homed in on Subha Sundaram's Shubha News and Photo Agency, a hotbed of pro-LTTE DK sympathizers in Madras. Prabhakaran reached out directly to Subha and asked him to help Muthuraja. Muthuraja, in turn, scouted among the photographers that Subha had on call, and picked Haribabu and another photographer, who were entrusted with housing and training a 'guest' who was coming in from Jaffna.

Haribabu became an enthusiastic member of the Muthuraja circle after he was paid handsomely; he even befriended the 'guest', Balan, who would convert him to their cause.

Next, 'Baby' Subramaniam recruited a young DK supporter, the penniless Bhagyanathan, along with his sister, Nalini, and his mother, Padma, a nurse employed at a local nursing home, who were soon to be evicted from their quarters, and were desperate for financial assistance. 'Baby' Subramaniam 'sold' his printing press to Bhagyanathan for a paltry Rs 5000 and the entire family moved into their new home at the press. Subramaniam had his captive audience—both for the virulently anti-Rajiv Gandhi propaganda that had to be printed and which the family would be subjected to and brainwashed into believing, and as the perfect hideout when 'friends' came visiting from Jaffna.

Nalini was given charge of editing and producing *Satanic Forces: Heinous Crimes of the Indian Peace Keeping Force*. This was a 3000-page collection of anti-India articles that would turn the young woman into a fierce critic of Rajiv Gandhi and a willing accomplice to the murder.

Sivaresan and Murugan, meanwhile, were still in Jaffna. They needed two youngsters who were adept at working transmitters and computers, and homed in on LTTE cadres Jayakumar and Payas from Udippidy, Sivaresan's home town in Jaffna. The two were dispatched to Madras in February, to the Porur home of Jayakumar's brother-in-law, Perarivalan, on the outskirts of the city. Perarivalan, the LTTE electronic genius, had been sent to Madras from Kilinochchi a year ago, without anyone in Indian intelligence aware of his true capabilities.

When Murugan arrived in mid-February, loaded with cash and weapons, all that Perarivalan was told was that he had a major attack to plan for: he was to construct a belt-bomb from explosives and RDX. They soon found a third safe house where Payas and Jayakumar were then ensconced, and equipped with a scooter bought with a fake licence. By then, Murugan too was brought into the Bhagyanathan circle by Muthuraja and became an integral member of the family, growing especially close to Nalini.

'Baby' Subramaniam and Muthuraja had, in the space of eight weeks, not only co-opted an Indian Tamil family to their cause, but set up three safe houses, activated a rogue radio operator and the man who could construct the bomb that the suicide bomber would use. All they needed now was the suicide bomber.

On 1 March, after receiving Murugan's report on the arrangements that had been put in place, Sivaresan landed at Kodiakkarai on the east coast of Tamil Nadu, not far from Nagapattinam. He headed for the safe house in Porur where Perarivalan's belt-bomb design was still only on paper.

Sivaresan set the wheels in motion to acquire the explosives, falling back on the same source from whom he had acquired the bombs to fell Padmanabha—KP, the LTTE's infamous arms procurer and chief financier, who, over the next month, would smuggle in 1 kilo of RDX as well as the deadly pellets from a factory in Singapore, which were finally used in the bomb.

Sivaresan moved into Bhagyanathan's home. He spun the web tighter around the five Indians and the three Lankan Tamils who were in on the conspiracy that had been forged in such secrecy in Prabhakaran's headquarters in Jaffna, little more than six months ago.

By the last week of March, 'Baby' Subramaniam and Muthuraja—their part of the mission accomplished—headed back to Jaffna, while Sivaresan would return in early April to brief Prabhakaran and Pottu Amman on the arrangements that were in place. Pleased, the LTTE chief is reported to have asked that the dry run and the actual assassination be recorded. This proved to be a fatal error.

Meanwhile, either in an elaborate ploy to lull Rajiv Gandhi into a false sense of complacency or gauge for himself where his true intentions lay, the LTTE supremo would send out the first of three emissaries.

The first was on 5 March 1991, when Rajiv Gandhi met a senior member of the LTTE's central committee, Kasi Anandan, at his 10, Janpath home in New Delhi. The meeting was held at the initiative of the LTTE and was put out as the first move by the Tigers to mend fences with the Indian leader whom they had publicly vilified for ordering the Indian Army into Sri Lanka's north and east in 1987, effectively foiling their armed struggle for a separate state.

One of the men who helped facilitate the meeting between Kasi and Rajiv Gandhi would later tell me how the backchannels between India and Sri Lanka had been actively trying to forge a truce between the LTTE and the former prime minister.

Kasi, who lives in a tiny rural township off the highway on the outskirts of Chennai—eerily close to Sriperumbudur—is a more than gracious host when I land at his doorstep in early 2015.

His home is tucked away from the main road and there is no nameplate announcing his presence, but the mason working on a house just around the corner knows exactly where Kasi lives. He points us in the right direction, calling to the long-haired Sri Lankan as he waits for us at the corner: 'Your guests have arrived.'

Accompanying me is a man that Kasi trusts implicitly and he opens up with ease in his presence, talking of how the Tiger leader wanted him to go and meet Rajiv Gandhi, to ascertain that there would be no repeat of 1987, no sending Indian troops into Sri Lanka to destroy the Tigers again.

As his daughter bustles around brewing tea, Kasi strongly refutes the imputation that it was his report on the meeting that set off the assassination. The message he sent to Prabhakaran was that Rajiv Gandhi, whose victory in the 1991 elections seemed certain, would not interfere in Sri Lanka during his second tenure.

'Even the officers investigating Rajiv Gandhi's assassination were given access to my report. They know what I have said,' said the earnest Kasi, bristling at the charge, as he talks about how he shared details of that conversation with *The Hindu*'s owner-editors as well as the SIT team once the investigation into the killing began.

At the time, though, none of the security agencies was privy to Kasi's meeting with the former prime minister, and there is no record of when he was secretly brought from New Delhi's Ashok Hotel to 10, Janpath. It may have taken place at the behest of Prabhakaran himself, no doubt, using the multiple connections he had with politicians and journalists in Madras to his advantage.

From Kasi's home, which even today is a virtual shrine to Prabhakaran, lined with oil lamps and a bank of photographs with the Tiger leader and his own brother, an LTTE martyr, the Tiger emigre says, 'I told him that contrary to reports that appeared in the newspapers that had Rajiv Gandhi saying he was going to send troops back to Sri Lanka, Rajiv Gandhi himself personally assured me that he had no intention of doing so.'

In fact, Kasi may have only speeded up plans for the assassination.

Prabhakaran was so furious when he received Kasi's report which said it was time to forget the past and open a new chapter with Rajiv Gandhi, that he not only tore it up in anger, but immediately gave the green signal to his deputy, Col Kittu, and the deputy leader of the women's wing, Akila, to put plans for the assassination into motion.

Prabhakaran was convinced that Kasi's judgement was completely off the mark. He sent a message to the London-based Kittu to find a way to get close to his RAW source in Delhi and suss out the real thinking of the Congress leader. Little more than a week later on 14 March 1991, Prabhakaran sent another team of LTTE officials through Col Kittu to meet the former Indian premier, along with a Tiger emissary who had also been flown in by Kittu from the United Kingdom. This was London-based financier Arjuna Sittampalam, who had been brought to see the former Indian premier through the intervention of his trusted Foreign Secretary Romesh Bhandari. This is when the LTTE operatives reportedly let it be known that they posed no threat to him and would never act against India, and encouraged him to campaign in Tamil Nadu.

Rajiv Gandhi, in turn, made solicitous inquiries about Prabhakaran's health and sought details on how the ground situation was and where Colombo's plans to devolve power to the north, now stood. It was, in fact, Sittampalam who correctly gauged Rajiv Gandhi's intentions, and would signal how little the LTTE should trust Rajiv Gandhi.

In a third meeting a fortnight later, on 28 March, of which there is no official record at all, barring an entry in the visitors book by his personal secretary, V. George, Rajiv Gandhi met Rajarattinam, the Delhi-based representative of the Eelam National Democratic Liberation Front (ENDLF). Rajiv Gandhi, who perceived Rajarattinam as being anti-LTTE, not fully realizing that the ENDLF shared the LTTE's goal of setting up an Ilankai Eelam, let his guard down. He was much more vocal and open at that meeting, freely airing his views that Prabhakaran and the LTTE were a group that he could never fully endorse. Word of the conversation between the two men trickled back to the LTTE chief.

Prabhakaran may have pulled the wool over Rajiv Gandhi's eyes, but there was no fooling the LTTE supremo.

By April 1991, the hunt for a suicide bomber had begun in earnest. When Akila reportedly suggested that it would be easier to smuggle a woman assassin into an election rally than a man, Prabhakaran was sold on the idea. Sivaresan soon homed in on his own kin, two of his cousins, both trained Tigresses fiercely committed to the cause—Dhanu and Subha.

On 1 May 1991, Sivaresan returned to India with a squad of nine, including the two young women who were taken to Nalini's home. A third, Athirai, had already been sent to Delhi as a fallback option after her arrival on 1 March. The third woman and the Delhi route was Pottu Amman's idea. Athirai was sent in the company of an old LTTE hand, Kanakasabapathy, who stayed in a house in Delhi's Moti Bagh, which belonged to Tamil politician Vaiko's associate. Vaiko, incidentally, was never questioned on the help he gave Prabhakaran's associate, and the SIT only questioned him as a 'witness' and not a conspirator in the plot to assassinate the former premier.

None of them knew that the target was Rajiv Gandhi, and were under the impression that it was Varadaraja Perumal, the EPRLF leader.

Perarivalan, meanwhile, was told the bomb would be made up of six 80-gm RDX grenades, armed with

2000 splinters, and charged with a 9-mm battery with two toggle switches. It had to be secreted into a denim vest, and a woman would be wearing it. The tailor who stitched the denim garment had no idea what it was meant for.

All that remained were the trial runs. The first was on 21 April at Marina Beach in Madras at Rajiv Gandhi's first campaign meeting in Tamil Nadu, which was also addressed by AIADMK leader Jayalalitha. A video and photographs record the event, where the women bombers had no role to play as they had not yet arrived in the city. The second was on 12 May, at a meeting addressed by V.P. Singh and Karunanidhi of the DMK at Thiruvallur in Arkonam, 40 kilometres from Madras. This time, Dhanu was present and the young woman, in a macabre rehearsal, practised the gesture she would repeat with Rajiv Gandhi on the fateful night of 21 May—by bending down and touching Singh's feet.

Ragothaman has an interesting take on the date and venue of the rally where Rajiv Gandhi's end would come. 'Few knew about Rajiv Gandhi's Sriperumbudur halt as the original itinerary prepared on 13 May 1991 by Congress leader Margaret Alva, his tour manager, did not include the town. The change in Rajiv Gandhi's poll itinerary to include Sriperumbudur was made at the last minute after Margatham Chandrashekhar, who was the party candidate there, urged him to campaign for her.

Rajiv Gandhi had jotted down in his own writing the change in itinerary, "Include Aunty's (as Margatham was called by the Gandhis) constituency also, but only for a day," he wrote.'

Sivaresan wouldn't find out Rajiv Gandhi was coming to Sriperumbudur until the Tamil newspaper *Dinatanthi* put out the news, barely twenty-four hours before the 21 May rally.

Sivaresan knew this was his opportunity, his best and his last chance, before polls wound up. As he arrived at Nalini's home with a copy of the popular Tamil daily on the morning of 20 May, it was decided: Sriperumbudur it would be.

On the night of 20 May, the co-conspirators watched a movie and seemed calm, as if the next day would be just another ordinary day. The women watched Dhanu as she tried on the vest-bomb and the outsized glasses that would help mask her face. At 4.30 p.m. on 21 May, Dhanu and Subha, along with Nalini and Sivaresan, left for Parry's Corner where Haribabu, the photographer, was waiting. He had been sent to buy the sandalwood garland from the state handicrafts store, Poompuhar, and was waiting for them, armed with a borrowed Chinon camera and a Konica colour roll.

No one looked twice at the group of five as they caught the bus to Sriperumbudur; they were just some election groupies going to the main event in town. They arrived at 8 p.m., an hour before Rajiv Gandhi landed in Madras, piloting his own plane from Visakhapatnam.

At the venue, they attracted the attention of an alert lady cop who asked them to move out of the VIP enclosure and the red carpet that was being rolled out, as Rajiv Gandhi wasn't due there for several hours.

In fact, Anasuya, the sub-inspector, questioned a day after the assassination, would identify the five and confirm that they had come together as a group. Asked what they were doing there, Haribabu told Anasuya he was there to take pictures of the girl garlanding Rajiv Gandhi. The sub-inspector shooed them away.

Subha and Nalini, and Sivaresan who was armed with a gun to finish the job if Dhanu didn't succeed, moved away, leaving Dhanu and Haribabu near the red carpet in the so-called 'sanitized area' on which Rajiv Gandhi would walk on his way to the dais.

Rajiv Gandhi arrived just after 10 p.m. and was immediately mobbed by Congress supporters trying to garland him and present him with silk scarves.

Seeing Dhanu approach, Anasuya stepped in front of her, grabbed her arm in a bid to prevent her from getting close to Rajiv Gandhi, and had almost succeeded in turning her away, when Rajiv Gandhi said: 'Let everybody get a chance.' Anasuya stepped back. Dhanu bent down to touch Rajiv Gandhi's feet. Rajiv Gandhi bent to lift her up. Dhanu activated the bomb.

The message that a grim Prabhakaran received on the wireless later that night, sent by Payas, was, 'Operation Wedding successful.'

The Jaffna Conspiracy had been executed to the satisfaction of the LTTE chief.

~

Within twenty-four hours, other Tamil militant groups housed in camps across Tamil Nadu—the Eelam People's Democratic Party (EPDP), the EPRLF and Tamil Eelam Liberation Organisation (TELO)—laid the blame squarely at Prabhakaran's door.

The LTTE's London headquarters and its spokesperson in Jaffna were uncharacteristically vigorous in their denial of any involvement in the assassination.

Anyone and everyone who tracked the Tigers was surprised, therefore, when on 25 May, four days after Rajiv Gandhi was assassinated, a report appeared in *The Hindu* which attempted to reinforce the LTTE denial, presenting a reasoned argument as to why the Tigers had no reason to kill him.

The report—which was clearly an LTTE plant—claimed that there was a 'reassessment of the role of Rajiv Gandhi by the LTTE', and a recognition on the part of the outfit that the 'withdrawal . . . allowed Colombo to resort with impunity to a military solution, all the promises of devolution to the Tamil people . . . falling in a heap by the wayside.'

The concluding paragraph read, 'The LTTE had seen for itself that Rajiv Gandhi was not hostile to it and that discovery presented a positive opening in political terms. The indications that the LTTE seemed to be placing its stakes on the return of Rajiv Gandhi to power would militate against a hasty conclusion that the militant group had an interest in killing Rajiv Gandhi, just two months after the wounded relationship between the LTTE and Rajiv Gandhi had been put on a friendlier footing.'

The LTTE, as always, at its best when it was muddying the message!

4

The Tamil Card—Strategy or Blunder?

AT THE HEIGHT OF THE Sri Lankan crisis in the 1980s and 1990s, all the major players in that country accused India of attempting to destabilize its smaller neighbour by arming Tamil separatists. And they continued to hold on to this belief through all the finger-pointing and accusations that followed. So the central question that must be addressed is this: Why did India under Indira Gandhi prepare for a covert intervention, only for her son and successor, Rajiv Gandhi, to abandon the Tamil card and, by accident or design, turn a strategic asset into an enemy?

Was India's Sri Lanka policy driven by these two Indian leaders personally? Or was it their advisers who altered their thinking on this unquiet island and, once that happened, sent relations between the two countries into a downward spiral?

Clearly, Indira and Rajiv Gandhi lived in different times and were governed by vastly differing strategic imperatives. They were also two individuals who looked at foreign policy through different prisms. Either way, history would show that neither of the paths chosen by the two leaders fully served Indian interests.

One talked war but never waged it; the other talked peace but went to war.

In the long run, arming the Tamil insurgents would prove to be counter-productive as it gave angry young Tamil men and women who had an axe to grind against the Sinhalas access to arms and weaponry they would not have had otherwise.

India failed to factor in that even if it shut off the arms tap, the Tamils had enough middlemen—Sri Lankan Tamil, Indian and foreign—to procure weapons through alternative sources.

Leaving the Tamil insurgents stranded, without the promised Tamil Eelam and with a province instead of a nation, alienated not just the Tamils—whose cause Delhi claimed it was espousing—but the Sri Lankan majoritarian polity as well. The overt Indian military intervention only served to reinforce the suspicions of an already wary Sinhala community that India was not there to play honest broker, but was preparing to midwife a de facto Tamil state.

Today, India–Sri Lanka relations are picking up after nearly forty years of mutual suspicion fuelled by one self-inflicted wound after another. But even six years after the LTTE was annihilated by the Mahinda Rajapaksa government in May 2009, Colombo was unable to fully embrace Delhi, at least not until the present government's new power trio—President Maithripala Sirisena, Prime Minister Ranil Wickremesinghe and former President Chandrika Bandaranaike Kumaratunga—recognized the perils of not having India fight their corner, especially when they were facing an international community more than ready to try them for war crimes.

But in the early 1980s, insiders say, Indira Gandhi, astute tactician that she was, let the Sri Lankan government know that she opposed their antithetical stance towards the Tamils and that she was more than ready to invade ethnically divided Sri Lanka in August 1984, if the need arose. The small army of Tamil militants at home was her fallback, the weapon that she would unleash when the time was right, just as she had done with the Mukti Bahini in Bangladesh.

The parallels—so far as the provocation for such a strike is concerned—between Bangladesh and Sri Lanka were tellingly similar. In 1971, a million or more Bengalis of Pakistani nationality, had escaped the genocidal Pakistani army and taken refuge in India, clearing the way for Mrs Gandhi to invade then East Pakistan and restore it to the Bengalis.

Similarly, following the anti-Tamil pogrom of 1983 that raged on until 1985, thousands of Sri Lankan Tamils abandoned their homes in the north and east of the deeply divided island, crossed the 18-kilometre stretch of the

Palk Strait in rickety boats and flooded into Tamil Nadu where they were settled in refugee camps all along the coast. They were clamouring for justice, for restitution. The then Tamil Nadu chief minister, Ramachandran, and Opposition DMK leader Karunanidhi were being pressed by Indian Tamils to save the Jaffna Tamils.

But there were crucial differences between this situation and that of East Pakistan. The Mukti Bahini had no rival Bengali groups to compete for India's affections. And unlike the Tamil Tigers, the East Pakistanis were true partners who went to war arm in arm with the Indian Army. Secondly, the Bengalis were being given a nation; the Tamils were told they had to be content with a truncated province—the north without the east. Indeed, Rajiv Gandhi never wanted the Tigers to become the sole voice of the Lankan Tamils and had always planned to give groups like the Tamil United Liberation Front (TULF) and the EPRLF an equal say.

Colombo's charge was that Indian interventionism was an all too real threat, in keeping with a pattern of intercessions in the neighbourhood, which began with East Pakistan in 1971 and was followed by the takeover of Sikkim in 1975. This, they felt, became a reality when Rajiv Gandhi used the ploy of 'Tamils in peril' to send troops into Sri Lanka in 1987.

Whether or not India genuinely believed it could solve the Sinhala–Tamil impasse or was sucked into a trap set by Sri Lankan President Jayewardene, few believe today that Indian boots landed on Lankan soil solely at the express invitation of the President of the island nation as J.N. Dixit, Rajiv Gandhi's pointman in Colombo, claims, both in his books *India's Foreign Policy*[1] and *Assignment Colombo*,[2] and in many interviews about the conversation between the two leaders he had been privy to.

Except, military escalation, especially when the firepower is foreign, comes with its own baggage. The results are never what you bargained for. The foreigner, in this case, the Indian Army—and Prime Minister Rajiv Gandhi—were, unfortunately, tarred as the barbarians at the gate.

Could Dixit, mentor and guide to so many journalists, including myself, have been trying to be economical with the truth on the reasons behind Rajiv Gandhi's decision to send troops into Sri Lanka?

The accusation that India was training and arming militants wasn't too far off the mark. Sri Lankan commentator Rohan Gunaratna in his searing book *Indian Intervention in Sri Lanka*,[3] published by the South

---

[1] J.N. Dixit, *India's Foreign Policy—Challenge of Terrorism Fashioning Interstate Equations* (New Delhi: Gyan Books, 2003).

[2] J.N. Dixit, *Assignment Colombo* (New Delhi: Konark Publishers, 1998).

[3] Rohan Gunaratna, *Indian Intervention in Sri Lanka* (Colombo: South Asian Network on Conflict Research, 1993).

Asian Network on Conflict Research, states that as many as 10,000 Tamil insurgents were being trained by India in thirty-odd training camps across Tamil Nadu and in the foothills of the Himalayas. He backs up the charge with pictorial evidence. This has of course never been acknowledged by the Indian government, as the training was allegedly conducted by servicemen recruited by the covert RAW, and not the army per se, giving all actors plausible deniability.

Apart from the LTTE, five other militant groups were created and given arms, training and funding. These included the TELO led by Sri Sabaratnam who was fully backed by Karunanidhi's DMK, the PLOTE, the Eelam Revolutionary Organization of Students (EROS), the EPRLF and the precursor to all these groups, the TELA.

India's abrupt scrapping of its covert policy of supporting Tamil separatists when Rajiv Gandhi became prime minister caused tremendous heartburn and anger among the Lankan Tamil community. Smuggling of weapons into Jaffna came to a halt as the coast guard stepped up patrolling soon after Rajiv Gandhi was told that an aircraft carrying weapons bound for Sri Lanka's Tamil-held north had been detained at Madras airport.

But Rajiv Gandhi's Sri Lanka policy, crafted at the height of the Cold War, was seen by him and his new team of advisers as pragmatic, equitable and as the need of the hour, even if it ultimately proved to be impractical and unenforceable. India's strategic interests were as much an issue for Rajiv Gandhi as they were for his mother and predecessor, but it was overlaid in his case by a well-meaning intent to start with a clean slate.

Mrs Gandhi's fondness for former premier Sirimavo Bandaranaike and the mutual hostility between her and Bandaranaike's successor, the Sri Lankan President Jayewardene, were the other mitigating factors behind the tough line she took on Sri Lanka's actions against its Tamil minority. But the critical factor in Mrs Gandhi's case may have been Indian intelligence agencies reporting that the US was pushing for a base in Trincomalee port, and setting up a powerful transmitter for its Voice of America radio station in the eastern port city that would enable it to snoop on India.

While it was an open secret that Delhi had been playing footsie with Tamil militants since 1981, Colombo's growing closeness to the US, Israel and Pakistan during that period required a plan to pull the strategically positioned island back into its sphere of influence.

Gen. Vernon Walters of the US, during his diplomatic forays into Sri Lanka in 1983–84, muddied the waters considerably with his attempt to co-opt Colombo by reportedly offering Israeli training and arms to the Sri Lankan armed forces as a quid pro quo for intelligence on India's Tamil assets. British mercenaries, under the cover of a private security firm, the oddly named Keenie Meenie

Services—'snake in the grass' in Swahili—were also active on the east coast.

Mrs Gandhi was equally concerned that the US' Cold War ally, arch-rival Pakistan, was similarly—much before the Chinese string of pearls strategy to encircle India—building bridges with the Sri Lankans, with many of its top officers training its army. At the height of the Bangladesh war in 1971, Colombo had alienated India by giving Pakistan's air force permission to refuel its aircraft and use its airfields, when India had closed off its airspace to Pakistan's civilian and military aircraft.

When Rajiv Gandhi became prime minister, the revolving door in his foreign policy cell also saw the exit of one seasoned expert after another who had been handling Colombo, including G. Parthasarathy (senior) and A.P. Venkateswaran, and the entry of Natwar Singh and P. Chidambaram as well as Arun Nehru and Arun Singh—the last two were unfamiliar with realpolitik. This happened even as Tamil Nadu Chief Minister Ramachandran kept lines open with the Lankan Tamil groups that he nurtured in the state.

Much before Rajiv Gandhi became aware of the Sri Lankan government's persistent foot-dragging over reaching an agreement with the Tamils, he had quickly come round to the belief that continuing support for Tamil separatists was no longer morally tenable. Pakistan's military establishment was still smarting from the humiliating defeat it suffered at the hands of the Indian Army in 1971 when it surrendered and 90,000 of its soldiers were taken prisoner. Islamabad was looking to settle scores with India.

With Pakistan readying plans to actively foment and support a separatist insurgency in Jammu and Kashmir, any move by India to prop up a militant movement would be used by Islamabad as ammunition in its stepped-up campaign to separate Kashmir from the Indian Union as payback for India's vivisection of Pakistan. Rajiv Gandhi was of the firm belief that India would have no locus standi over Jammu and Kashmir if it was seen as backing a claim to a separate state by Sri Lankan rebels whom it supported and funded.

Equally important, he wanted to end, once and for all, the pipe dream of a Tamil Desam that was being actively promoted by India's canny Tamil politicians who at the time (much as they do today) used the plight of the Sri Lankan Tamils to weaken his Congress party.

The pan-Tamil state would bring together Tamil Nadu on the Indian mainland, the Tamil 'homeland' in Sri Lanka's north and east, and parts of Malaysia and Singapore in South East Asia, where a sizeable Tamil-speaking population resided. In sending Indian troops to Sri Lanka, therefore, Rajiv Gandhi was signalling unequivocally that India would no longer back the Tamil insurgents in their quest to create an independent 'Greater Eelam'. What he hadn't been able to do was convince Colombo that India had no intention of taking over northern Sri Lanka as a prelude to creating a separate state for the Tamils, and that the 'interference' of sending in the IPKF was only to ensure that Tamils were not persecuted thereafter. Rajiv Gandhi wanted to be seen as a 'guarantor' of peace and not as an invader, or the head of an army of occupation.

Rajiv Gandhi's Sri Lanka policy—a reversal of Mrs Gandhi's militaristic line—was in keeping with the rejection of many of Indira Gandhi's other policies, demonstrated by the Rajiv Gandhi–Longowal accord in Punjab and the Assam accord. In April 1987, with Bofors casting a shadow over his prime ministership, former diplomat Ambassador K.C. Singh says the commonly held view, as the scam blew up in Rajiv Gandhi's face, was that he was probably looking for a foreign policy success that would take attention away from the controversial howitzer deal. 'The Indo-Sri Lankan accord that Rajiv Gandhi pushed the Sri Lankan President into agreeing to, was going to be it,' says Singh.

Rajiv Gandhi, temperamentally different from his mother, did not want to go down in history as being politically incorrect and as having meddled in the affairs of another nation. His advisers may even have put it about that forging peace with Sri Lanka after a slew of accords with insurgents at home could win him the Nobel Peace Prize, alongside Sri Lankan President Jayewardene.

~

Rajiv Gandhi's Bid to Solve the Ethnic Impasse

There is no doubt that solving the ethnic impasse in Sri Lanka was a major challenge for the young prime minister, faced with multiple foreign policy crises.

In 1984, the LTTE had not yet become the formidable guerrilla force that it would eventually grow into. Indeed, it was just one of many that India had in play. Its chief, Prabhakaran, befriended by Tamil Nadu leaders like the iconic MGR, with whom he shared ethnic linkages (their fathers came from Kerala, India, and took up work in Sri Lanka's plantations), was the only Tamil insurgent leader who made no secret of his reservations about the accord.

Flown to Delhi in July 1987, and kept incommunicado in a room at Ashok Hotel until he agreed to go along with the accord (he had sat on it for almost two hours, after which it was translated from English to Lankan Tamil), he finally extracted a verbal promise of monetary help for his cadres from Rajiv Gandhi when they met late that night, and believed that of all the Tamil groups supported by Delhi, he was the one who would be given the lead role in the Northern and Eastern provinces.

But Prabhakaran must have known that he had nothing on paper. Ill-advisedly, he was allowed access to a telephone.

In a phone call to Tamil Nadu politician Vaiko, Prabhakaran gave vent to his fears when he said, 'We have been betrayed.' A phrase that he would raise at the first public rally he ever addressed, on his return to Jaffna in August 1987, and again and again over the next few weeks and months, whipping up emotions until he went to war with the IPKF.

Prabhakaran had dug in his heels over talking to Colombo, resisting the pressure to agree to a negotiated peace settlement when he had been flown to the SAARC summit in Bangalore in 1986. It was in Bangalore that the newly elected Indian prime minister first shared with Sri Lankan President Jayewardene his concerns over the escalating ethnic violence in Sri Lanka and the difficulties posed in hosting armed Tamil militants on Indian soil. But Jayewardene reportedly did not play along and was openly critical of India at the SAARC meet.

This deeply upset Rajiv Gandhi's advisers, possibly forcing the Indian leader's hand on pushing Jayewardene into agreeing to the broad contours of an agreement that, at one level, served Colombo's purpose as it brought India in to tackle the Tamil insurgents they had nurtured, while ensuring that India could not back Tamil terror outfits. Rajiv Gandhi believed that at least on paper, he had a victory as the accord made it incumbent on the Sri Lankan leadership to give the Tamils a status within a sovereign, united Sri Lanka.

However, as a former diplomat said, Rajiv Gandhi was also being cautioned by his Tamil allies and his military and intelligence advisers against allowing Jaffna to fall to the Sri Lanka Army. It would take away one of India's few bargaining chips—control of Jaffna—and scupper the rehabilitation of Tamils who were resentful of being treated like second-class citizens in their own country, the grudge that was at the heart of the insurgency. In fact, during Operation Liberation in May 1987, Sri Lankan forces had already captured the LTTE nerve centre of Vadamarachchi and were within a heartbeat of taking Jaffna.

The paradox was that without the Tiger 'gun' being held to their head, Colombo would have not have brought the real power behind the Tamil insurgents, the lumbering Indian elephant, into the room. Equally, in conceding on an intervention, Rajiv ceded the upper hand to Colombo and boxed himself into a corner. He could no longer deliver on the promises he had made to Prabhakaran who had serious misgivings about the accord, particularly the call for a referendum on the Eastern Province, that was nothing more, he believed, than a ploy to divide the north and the east.

Prabhakaran had no intention of revisiting the merger of the north and east, calling it a fait accompli.

The deliberate resettlement by Colombo of the Sinhalese-speaking southerners in the Eastern Province, with the armed forces bringing in their families and moving into homes in the area once occupied by Tamils, had left the returning Tamil population without a roof over their head in their traditional homeland. Prabhakaran believed the referendum was an intentional move to change the demographics and reverse the unification of the north and the east.

In interviews to various publications in August 1987, after the Indian Army had flown him from India to Jaffna ahead of a public surrender of arms planned for early October, Prabhakaran said as much. 'Having fought so much, having sacrificed so many lives and having lost 20,000 people, all this has been subordinated to India's strategic interests. Not only that, we, the representatives of such martyrs, have not been properly respected. Hence, in this kind of situation during the interim arrangement . . . we feel that we want to demonstrate to the Government of India the support we have from the people. India has not given us our due.

'Without consulting us, they have arrived at an agreement. Hence, we would like to enter politics with the people's support and with the goal of Tamil Eelam. That will be the fitting reply.'

In the same interview to an Indian publication, Prabhakaran was asked what Rajiv Gandhi's response was when the LTTE supremo raised the issue of the removal of the 200 Sri Lankan army camps that had been set up across Trincomalee and Batticaloa. 'We oppose the agreement on this point. Nobody was prepared to consider it,' he said. In Delhi, the interviewer asked. 'Yes, in Delhi,' replied Prabhakaran.

In forcing Prabhakaran to return to Jaffna, India also failed to factor in that the militant leader, for the first time since he had taken up arms, was having to resolve the day-to-day problems of the people whose cause he was claiming to espouse. Hundreds of Lankan Tamils could not return to their own homes that had been commandeered by the Sri Lankan settlers from the south, and the only person he could blame this on was the Indian prime minister.

As he told the interviewer: 'Mr Rajiv Gandhi gave the assurance that we, the Tamil people, will be protected in the north and the east. But people are not able to return to the east . . . The Indian Army has gone there but the Tamil people are not able to go there—because there is an increasing opposition from the Sinhalese Home Guards and the Sinhalese people. There are army camps there in individual houses, schools and cooperative stores. But the Indian Army has not been deployed in such places. The Ceylon Army has not been evacuated, the problem has not been solved. Another thing is the people's lack of faith arising out of the non-removal of the Ceylon Army. Even if the Indian Army goes, occupies such places and later vacates, the Sinhala army will come back. Further, we wouldn't have arms.'

In fact, the forced surrender of arms would blow up in India's face. An LTTE representative told Tamil newspaper *Uthayan* in Jaffna that the organization would not surrender their arms. Prabhakaran reconfirmed it in several interviews to Indian newspapers, including *Indian Express* and *Frontline*. 'Yes, we made the statement. It is better to fight and die than surrender the weapons in an insecure environment and die on a mass scale.'

The idea of sending troops into Sri Lanka may have been raised by the Sri Lankan President first. But lulled into a false sense of confidence by Rajiv Gandhi's assurances that India would not betray Tamil interests, it took several weeks before it finally dawned on the LTTE that India had turned its back on them.

The other Tamil separatists were far more accepting of the new reality in the hope that it would be their turn to be at the receiving end of RAW largesse in the near future. However, for the LTTE, in the forefront of the battle for Eelam, their very survival was at stake. Caught on the wrong foot, Prabhakaran and his cadres who knew no other language but confrontation and war, retaliated the only way they knew how.

If Rajiv Gandhi is to be blamed, it should be for his political naivety and for not heeding the advice of his outspoken and highly respected Foreign Secretary A.P. Venkateswaran.

Venkateswaran made no secret of his misgivings over sending Indian troops into Sri Lanka, saying in public that India's decision to send the IPKF to Sri Lanka was a mistake. He was dismissed by Rajiv Gandhi during a press conference in June 1987.

Foreign ministry officials who served at the time say that the momentous decision Rajiv Gandhi took, without considering his more seasoned advisers' concerns, was fraught with risk. It was made worse when there was no attempt to seek some kind of accommodation with the Tamil insurgents by offering a middle path, a face-saver that would give the proud Tamil primacy in a new arrangement, by holding out the promise of a state sometime in the future, however negligible the prospect of that ever coming to fruition.

Instead, critics say, he cut the most virulent—and potentially the most deadly—of the insurgent groups, the LTTE, out completely, seeing them as no different from the clutch of other Tamil separatists that India had propped up. Open to the highly manipulative suggestion of a far more adept politician in the Sri Lankan President, Rajiv Gandhi failed to examine the implications and the fallout of sending soldiers into unfamiliar terrain. They were, in the final analysis, being sent to do a job that should have rightfully been that of the Sri Lankan army.

Rajiv Gandhi's statement in Parliament, a day after the accord was signed, sought to justify the deployment to his domestic audience as well as to the international community. Someone should have told him that it would win him no plaudits either in the Sinhala or the Tamil camp.

In his own mind, it seems likely he had come to understand that the troops were going in as part of an agreement with the Sri Lankan government, and that it was aimed at disarming the Tamil militants, with the final goal being the devolution of powers to a Tamil-empowered council in the north and the east.

In his announcement in Parliament on 30 July 1987, he said:

President Jayewardene explained that because of the deteriorating situation as a result of [these] disturbances and the increasing demands that this puts on the Sri Lankan security forces, his government would need assistance to implement the Indo-Sri Lanka Agreement for ending the ethnic crisis. For this purpose the Government of Sri Lanka made a formal request for appropriate Indian military assistance to ensure the cessation of hostilities and surrender of arms in the Jaffna Peninsula, and if required, the Eastern Province ...

He also requested for air transport to move some of the Sri Lankan troops from Jaffna to points in the south. In response to this formal request from Government of Sri Lanka, and in terms of our obligations under the Indo-Sri Lanka Agreement, units of the Armed Forces of India have landed in the Jaffna Peninsula today [30 July 1987].

Let me repeat that our troops have landed in Sri Lanka in response to a specific and formal request of the Government of Sri Lanka who have invoked our obligations and commitments under the Indo-Sri Lanka Agreement . . .

As Dixit, then Indian high commissioner to Sri Lanka, said in an interview to Rediff's Josy Joseph in 2000, ten years after the IPKF withdrew from the island, the idea of Indian boots on the ground was Jayewardene's idea. Whether he was trying to shift the blame from Rajiv Gandhi, one will never know. But he said the idea of flying in Indian troops was 'a separate matter' from the accord itself, repeatedly stressing that it was not Rajiv Gandhi's idea. The Sri Lankan President, he said, had pushed Rajiv Gandhi to bring in troops to disarm the LTTE, as he wanted to free the Sri Lanka Army to quell a bloody Sinhala insurgency led by the Janata Vimukta Perumana (JVP) in the south.

'President Jayewardene wanted to withdraw his troops from Jaffna to control the riots in the south. And it was he who said, "I want some Indian troops to come in to ensure security in Jaffna and Trincomalee, because I am withdrawing my Sinhalese troops to maintain law and order here," Dixit recounted.

'And Mr Rajiv Gandhi—I was present—said, "Are you sure you want our troops? Because India can be criticised, Sri Lanka can be criticised." He [Jayewardene] said, "I am going to give you a formal written invitation." Mr Gandhi said, "Let us first sign the agreement, and then in your letter, if you think it is necessary, you say to ensure the efficient implementation of the agreement you want the troops." So it was a separate matter,' Dixit says.

Dixit's account of what actually transpired between the two leaders at the signing of the India–Sri Lanka peace accord underlined the Indian leader's ingenuousness and inexperience in dealing with Colombo.

Col Taylor (Retd) who served with the IPKF writes in Rediff.com of how LTTE cadres he later met told him: 'The cunning old fox fooled the innocent lamb.' No prizes for guessing who the lamb was and who, the fox.

What that meant in real terms was that India had been cleverly manoeuvred into doing the job that should have been entrusted to the Sri Lanka Army. The unpleasant task of defanging the rebels whom India had armed in the first place would now fall to Indian troops. Rajiv Gandhi was not prescient enough to foresee how unwelcome this would make Indian troops, how the terms of engagement would change for the worse and how catastrophic the consequences would be.

The primary challenge before the Indian troops was disarmament as a prelude to the elections. Unless the LTTE voluntarily surrendered their weapons or were forcibly disarmed by Indian troops, elections to the newly announced provincial councils could not take place. In effect, with the LTTE creating a climate of violence, a voluntary surrender of their weapons was not feasible; neither was disarmament nor were provincial polls.

One former soldier who served in the IPKF and did not want to be named, recounts the farcical disarmament. He said that when the order went out to the Tamil separatists to disarm, they were told to put all their firearms and equipment in the Jaffna Football Stadium. Pits were dug and, over several days until 21 August 1987, arms, most of them old, damaged and unusable, were brought in and buried. But in an indication of how little India understood what it was up against, the arms surrender stopped without warning, and when the IPKF went to check whether the stash was still intact, they found vast, empty pits. The story doing the rounds then, the former soldier said, was that with the LTTE suspicious of Indian intent to disarm the Tigers and arm rival Tamil groups, the outfit decided to hijack all the weapons and redistribute them among their own cadres.

What India had done was trade in Indira Gandhi's hard-nosed realpolitik-driven arming of Tamil insurgents that began in 1977 and went on till 1985—a year after she died—for Rajiv Gandhi's half-baked, midstream change of plan that went from attempting to divest the LTTE and other Tamil guerrillas of their firepower—which was a challenge in itself—to waging a full-fledged war against the Tigers.

Mrs Gandhi's strategy towards Sri Lanka was honed through the Cold War years when the US remained inimical to Indian interests, allying itself with Pakistan. With Sri Lanka located strategically at India's underbelly, President Jayewardene's increasingly strong relationship with Pakistan, the US and Israel was seen as a strategic threat that had to be countered. This was driven home as the British brought in hired mercenaries of various nationalities under the Keenie Meenie group to help train the Sri Lankan Task Force to quell the rebels in the east.

The risk posed by the secession-prone state of Tamil Nadu was also all too real. Tamil Nadu had about 60 million Tamil-speaking Indians who held Delhi to account for not speaking out or acting to alleviate the atrocities and marginalization of the Sri Lankan Tamils at the hands of the Sinhalese majority.

Mrs Gandhi was repeatedly asked by her Tamil allies why she had gone to war on behalf of the Bengalis but would not do the same for the Tamils.

Rajiv Gandhi's Lankan misadventure, his apologists say, was his bid to carry forward his mother's plans to their logical conclusion, by sending troops to the island to safeguard Lankan Tamil interests; except that in Mrs Gandhi's case, she used the Tamil groups to her advantage—the provisional fifth column that could be used against Colombo, if needed. That wasn't even a part of Rajiv Gandhi's calculations. And he capitulated, even though he held all the cards, said a colonel who had served in the IPKF. The Indian Armed Forces at the time were far superior to the Sri Lanka Army, and the LTTE could have remained a useful pawn if India had kept Prabhakaran's hopes of a separate state alive.

Instead, India rushed in peace-keeping forces that set off an undeclared war. Coming in as they did, completely unprepared and ill-equipped for the job at hand, the IPKF deployment set the seal on post-Independence India's biggest foreign policy disaster. In the years since, Indian policymakers have vowed never to repeat the misadventure.

Ironically, the Indo-Lanka peace accord pleased nobody in Colombo either. Senior members of the Jayewardene-led ruling United National Party (UNP) were not in favour of it, nor was the Opposition Sri Lanka Freedom Party (SLFP), much less the virulently anti-Tamil JVP which had set off the conflagration between the Tamils and the Sinhalese in the first place.

The 29 July accord that cleared the deployment of Indian troops to 'enforce the cessation of hostilities . . .' would unravel almost as soon as it became operational. The JVP, which had been assiduously fanning Sinhala ire at Indian interference in their internal affairs, stoked the first flames.

On the very day that the deal was signed, a failed attempt by a Sri Lankan naval rating to assassinate Rajiv

Gandhi—managing to hit him with his rifle butt—in full view of a guard of honour as senior members of the government in the Sri Lankan capital of Colombo watched, indicated the popular mood. It reflected the anger—which united Sinhalas and Tamils alike—and their collective antipathy to the arrival of foreign troops on their soil.

In Jaffna, the Indian premier's announcement in Parliament on 30 July that Indian troops were being air-dropped into Sri Lanka, even as he spoke, was particularly poorly received.

Once known for its genteel old-world charm, its bookshops, its voluble trishaw drivers, a famed university and a library that was the repository of ancient Tamil culture, Jaffna had by the mid-1980s turned into a hotbed of divisive, bloody Tamil separatist politics, marked by the rise of a highly motivated group committed to carving out a Tamil homeland.

Indian troops coming in with the express intent to disarm the LTTE in the north and the east, as a prelude to setting up an interim council and supervising elections to a provincial body, set off alarm bells in the terror outfit.

The Indian Army, since it divested Pakistan in 1971 of its East Bengal wing—a textbook success story that is taught in military schools across the world—had a formidable reputation. It believed it would be no pushover. Egged on by Dixit, the Tigers had reluctantly been persuaded to be a part of the interim council that would run the newly merged Northern and Eastern provinces. But, for Prabhakaran's cadres, compared by analysts to the fanatical and highly motivated Japanese kamikaze bombers, this was not the prize they sought.

The Indian Army, the Indian High Commission and RAW were blind to the fact that Prabhakaran's final frontier wasn't an interim government, let alone a Provincial Council. Prabhakaran didn't want a Colombo-inspired dispensation that would grant Tamil groups a voice. He wanted to be *the* pre-eminent voice, the only voice of the Tamil people, and he wanted it under a fully militarized force in a separate state, his state—Eelam. After years of exposure to Indian training camps in Tamil Nadu, he knew that the only thing that stood between him and Eelam was Rajiv Gandhi and his force majeure, the IPKF.

For the JVP, the deployment of the IPKF was a huge and unexpected bonus, a boost to their agenda to curb Tamil ambitions for a separate state.

Banned for the Black July 1983 racial pogrom against the Tamils—a retaliation for the killing of Sri Lankan soldiers and Buddhist monks—the JVP and its military arm, the Deshapremi Janatha Viyaparaya, seized the opportunity provided by Jayewardene (who had once promised to fight the Indians to the last bullet but ended up befriending them instead) to unleash a vitriolic campaign of hate against India and their own President for their so-called plans to 'divide' the island.

The accord that empowered the Indian Army to ensure power devolved to the northern and eastern Tamils enraged Sinhalese supremacists as it was seen as rewarding separatists who had taken up arms against the state.

On the morning that the Indo-Sri Lanka agreement was to be signed, an angry mob surrounded the President's home in Colombo; they attacked it and set it ablaze. In the run-up to the accord and after, the JVP began picking out leaders in predominantly Sinhala villages, both Catholic and Buddhist. They were given a choice: they had to come over to their side or they would be assassinated.

The huge outcry fomented by the JVP—and the Sri Lanka Freedom Party—grew into a mass movement against 'Indian imperialism' and 'Eelam terrorism', which began even before the first Indian soldier had set foot on Lankan soil. It wasn't helped by the fact that two senior ministers in the Jayewardene-led UNP government, Lalith Athulathmudali and Premadasa (both, incidentally, later assassinated), with one eye on the conservative Sinhala vote, were dead set against allowing even a limited measure of Tamil autonomy. Both leaders actively set out to sabotage the accord, while Premadasa went on to use it to unseat Jayewardene and assume power.

When Rajiv Gandhi stepped down from power in the face of the Bofors storm in 1989, the new prime minister

V.P. Singh and his foreign minister I.K. Gujral set out to reverse what Rajiv Gandhi had tried to do in Sri Lanka. But in withdrawing Indian troops under pressure from Sri Lanka's President Premadasa, a further complication had arisen.

As part of the sustained campaign by the LTTE against the 'foreign force', it was put out by the Tigers that on RAW's advice, Rajiv Gandhi had re-armed other insurgent groups, including the EPRLF, the ENDLF and the PLOTE. Flaunting newly acquired arms, yet inept at fighting the LTTE, they became easy targets of the LTTE's systematic elimination of the groups' leaders and cadres.

But in the counter-narrative that the Indians did little to play up, the LTTE was also flaunting brand new weapons. The IPKF officers believed the arms came from the pool of new weapons acquired by the Sri Lanka Army—they all had SLA markings. The Lankan charge against India was that it had armed and trained, and pitted one group of Tamils against another, so that one of their proxies would become powerful, and the Indian Army's charge against Premadasa was that he had done the same with the LTTE.

As Col Hariharan who served as India's chief of military intelligence in Sri Lanka during the IPKF's tenure from 1987 to 1990 explains, this was part of the LTTE's strategy to run the IPKF out of Sri Lanka. Instead of the three years that the IPKF had believed it would take them to 'neutralize' the LTTE, the Indian Army had within the space of two years 'wiped out most of the six levels of junior Tiger leaders'.

Col Hariharan told me the decimation of the LTTE mid-level cadres and the fear that he could get totally wiped out led Prabhakaran to 'run to Premadasa to get the IPKF out of the country', and form a bizarre alliance that united the LTTE and Premadasa against a shared enemy—the IPKF. Posters appeared in Colombo calling the IPKF 'Innocent People Killing Force'.

Doing business with the LTTE, however, always came with a price. In April 1993, after Premadasa had outlived his usefulness to the Tigers—and barely a week after his friend-turned-critic Athulathmudali, who had survived a terrible bomb attack on the Parliament, was shot dead by a gunman who Premadasa swore was sent by the LTTE—he himself would be blown up at a May Day rally by an LTTE suicide bomber.

India's Tamil card, flawed as it was, had already gone up in flames. Its newly acquired Sinhala card was doomed even before the ink had dried on the Indo-Lanka peace accord.

5

The RAW Truth

'RAJIV GANDHI AVARUNDE MANDALAI ADDIPODALAM.'
'Dump pannidungo.' Blow Rajiv Gandhi's head off. Eliminate him. *'Maranai vechidungo.'* Kill him.

Of the hundreds of intercepts between the thirty-eight-odd Tamil insurgent camps in the Nilgiris in India and their cohorts in Jaffna, Sri Lanka, almost every single one centred on arms shipments and gunrunning between Vedaranyam and Point Pedro, barely 18 kilometres from coast to coast. But no intercept would be as chilling as the kill order that came through in short bursts of VHS communication on a frequency that the LTTE favoured, that April day in 1990.

When it was intercepted, it set off alarm bells among Tamil insurgents ranged against the Tigers, their numbers already worn thin by the LTTE's targeting of their cadres and top leadership. The intercept, in Old Tamil interspersed with English used by the Jaffna Tamils—and largely incomprehensible to Indian Tamils—only added to the confusion that hung over the all too brief radio message.

'Dump'. That particular term came into use when the LTTE began to ruthlessly eliminate Tamil civilians who resisted their fiat and 'dumped' them in pits across Jaffna. It was another way of saying 'kill'.

But the difference this time was that the order was not to eliminate one of their own. The target was the former Indian prime minister, the leader of another country.

When PLOTE leader Siddharthan Dharmalingam first heard it, he was so alarmed, he immediately tipped off the IPKF's counter-intelligence head in Sri Lanka, Col Hariharan.

A native Tamil speaker with an inside track into the Lankan Tamil narrative, Col Hariharan was greatly helped in his task, he says, by having an aunt who was married to a Jaffna native. It was Col Hariharan, the head of Counter Intelligence (COIN), and one of a handful of Indian operatives with his ear to the ground and an understanding of the Tigers' mindset, who recognized its true import.

But it didn't fly. Whether it wasn't specific enough or clear enough to warrant immediate action, or was simply not taken seriously by the intelligence mandarins to whom the information was passed on, is not known. Either way, India's intelligence agents were clearly unequal to the task of reading the threat for what it was—a death sentence passed by the LTTE, an insurgent group nurtured by India, on India's former premier.

'Even when Rajiv Gandhi was the Prime Minister, the R&AW had drawn attention to the likelihood of a threat to his security from the Sri Lankan Tamil extremist organizations. It repeated this warning after he became the Leader of the Opposition,' says B. Raman, head of RAW during 1988–94, in his eye-popping memoir, *The Kaoboys of R&AW*.[1] 'These warnings did not receive the attention they deserved because they were based on assessments and not on specific intelligence,' he writes.

Except, this particular intercept was as specific as it could get.

Prabhakaran's 'handler' when the LTTE leader was in India, Chandran, is pushing eighty-five, but remembers the intercept as clearly as though it were yesterday. He recounts how everyone misread the signals—not just his men, but also agents from the IB who were tasked with monitoring the threat posed by Lankan Tamils residing in India, who had to trawl through hundreds of messages that went back and forth.

Chandran, additional secretary in the Cabinet Secretariat and in charge of RAW in Sri Lanka, was

---

[1] B. Raman, *The Kaoboys of R&AW: Down Memory Lane* (New Delhi: Lancer Publishers, 2007).

sidelined once the Rajiv Gandhi government fell, and his years of cultivating the Tamil militants came to nought.

'By that time, the government had changed. Nobody wanted to hear what we had to say anyway. And I had been shunted out,' he said.

'The IB and RAW didn't agree on much. If we had read the signals right, if we understood what was going on in Prabhakaran's mind, who knows, we could have prevented this. It was our fault, we made a huge error of judgement. We misread Prabhakaran. We never believed he would turn against us in this manner. We should have seen it coming. We didn't. We failed Rajiv Gandhi, we failed to save his life,' he said, emotional and close to tears as he spoke to me from his office in New Delhi.

Twenty-five years later, neither Siddharthan nor Col Hariharan remembers more than this particular part of the intercept. But both say that if it had been taken on board, and acted on with the seriousness that such a tip-off deserved, history would have taken a different course.

It was brought to the notice of Siddharthan (now a Tamil National Alliance MP in the newly elected Sri Lankan Parliament) by an alert Jaffna Tamil in his employ who monitored radio communications between Tamils on the Indian mainland and Jaffna. The PLOTE leader, in turn, alerted Col Hariharan who served in Sri Lanka from 3 August 1987 to June–July 1990 and was reaching the end of his tenure.

At the time, the LTTE was the predominant force in the RAW-run training camps in India. Col Hariharan who also had a small army of Jaffna Tamils keeping an eye on the LTTE for him, says he too was taken aback when he was given the cassette to listen to and, from what his code-breakers told him, was alarmed enough to warn India's IB that a plot was afoot to eliminate Rajiv Gandhi.

This was a full year before the suicide bomb blast claimed the former prime minister's life.

'It was the first time we heard any mention of Prabhakaran taking vengeance against Rajiv Gandhi,' Siddharthan said, quickly correcting himself after having first used the word 'revenge'.

But the warning—albeit tenuous and imprecise—instead of being investigated, was laughed out of court; it was simply set aside and forgotten.

It wasn't the only warning that wasn't fully investigated. In his book, Raman talks of another alert, this time from German intelligence, about the repeated visits of a Sri Lankan Tamil explosives expert and an LTTE sympathizer to Madras. But it was not sufficiently probed by the IB. Instead, it ignored the warning on the grounds that the Lankan Tamil wasn't an explosives expert, and remained curiously blind to the question of what the man was doing in Madras in the first place.

In 1990, LTTE had the upper hand. PLOTE's founder Maheswaran had co-founded the LTTE with Prabhakaran in 1976. But by 1982, the two had fallen out and almost killed each other in a public shoot-out in Madras. Maheswaran went on to found PLOTE but was murdered in broad daylight on a Colombo street in 1989.

PLOTE made every effort to stay one step ahead of the main person of interest at the time—their main enemy, 'Baby' Subramaniam, the LTTE commander operating out of Tamil Nadu. Subramaniam was the LTTE's point person to eliminate all challenges to Prabhakaran.

'Subramaniam was the darling of the Tamil Nadu politicians and knew exactly how to keep RAW and everyone happy while doing exactly what Prabhakaran wanted him to do,' Siddharthan tells me. The intercept may have been to Subramaniam from someone speaking on Prabhakaran's behalf. Together with other LTTE leaders, like the intelligence chief Pottu Amman and the deputy head of the women's wing, Akila, Subramaniam was closely involved with the planning and execution of the plot to kill Rajiv Gandhi.

Even though the Indian Army was making tracks for home, Prabhakaran was relentlessly whipping up anger against the IPKF, blaming them for excesses against civilians.

This single burst of chatter should have alerted the then V.P Singh government and, subsequently, the Chandrashekhar government to restore the Z security that Rajiv Gandhi used to have before he lost the prime ministership. Opposition leader or not, he was on the hit list of the Khalistanis and the Sikhs, and warranted more than the negligible cover he had been provided.

~

Rajiv Gandhi was too proud to ask for it, and his political opponents lacked the generosity of spirit to give it to him.

The PLOTE alert—which may or may not have changed their thinking—did not even reach the Prime Minister's Office. In fact, Col Hariharan said he had his knuckles rapped for raising the alarm about the plot to assassinate the former prime minister even though the intercept was nothing less than Prabhakaran putting a hit on Rajiv Gandhi.

'I was asked to stick to my brief,' Col Hariharan told me. The IPKF was after all, packing up to leave Sri Lanka, removing the main source of the grouse against Rajiv Gandhi. 'Politically, we had become unwanted baggage in both Colombo and New Delhi; our mandate was finished, we were on our way out. But RAW, overconfident of its influence over the LTTE, failed to factor in that revenge was always on the cards when it came to VP [Vellupillai Prabhakaran].'

Raman, commenting on the LTTE's poor communication security in his book, brings up the IB's 'better interception capability'—which gave them the ability to listen in on the Tigers—versus 'R&AW's better code breaking capability', while driving home the larger point of how little trust there was between the various agencies running India's biggest covert operation. He said the huge gaps left in the intelligence gathering on the Tamil groups, resulting from how little one agency knew about what the other was doing, did enormous damage to India's conduct of its Sri Lanka policy.

More fatally, 'The Monitoring Division failed to detect the conspiracy to kill Rajiv Gandhi before the tragedy took place,' says Raman. 'Sharing of knowledge of each other's capabilities—particularly in respect of intelligence collection—and joint or co-ordinated exploitation of these capabilities should be the norm if we have to avoid such surprises,' writes Raman, unsparing in his criticism of the agencies.

The critical intercept—a Tamil-speaking LTTE operative passing on the order to eliminate Rajiv Gandhi—was handed over by Col Hariharan to his old friend and IB additional director in Madras, the late K. Saranyan, within days of its receipt.

'I sent it to him, rather than defence HQ or army HQ, because our brief in Sri Lanka was over,' Col Hariharan said. 'We were winding up our interception ops and we no longer had jurisdiction or responsibility. Saranyan was a good friend and I respected him. But his assessment was that LTTE would never do it because they were so "stupid". I remember my response to him at that time: "My responsibility is over but I would never discount it just because the LTTE is stupid."'

Col Hariharan, on his way to his new posting in Jammu and Kashmir, never asked the IB official about it again. That's what he told the SIT when he was called in for questioning after Sriperumbudur. 'Nobody took it seriously because no one believed that a man who owed everything to India and Rajiv Gandhi would undertake an operation of this scale, his fanaticism and commitment to Eelam notwithstanding,' Hariharan tells me.

As the late Raman also pointed out in *Kaoboys*:

When there is such an assessment indicating the likelihood of a threat to a VVIP, the intelligence agencies are expected to initiate specific operations through their sources and through technical means to look for concrete indicators of such a threat. No such action was taken because everybody presumed—disastrously as it turned out—that, while the LTTE and other Sri Lankan Tamil organisations might indulge in acts of terrorism against each other in Indian territory, they would not indulge in acts of terrorism against any Indian leader.

The entire focus of the intelligence coverage of the LTTE was on its activities in Sri Lanka, its gun-running etc. There was no specific focus on likely threats to Rajiv Gandhi's security from it.

~

India's intelligence agencies comprehensively failed to pool their not inconsiderable resources and work together to manage and monitor what was its most ambitious and certainly its biggest clandestine operation since the Mukti Bahini in 1970–71. If proof was required, one needed to look no further than the mole within the LTTE that one Indian intelligence wing nurtured and no one outside that circle, nobody in MI on the ground, or the IB, knew about—Mahattaya, real name Gopalaswamy Mahendrarajah from Point Pedro.

The man was cultivated and positioned by RAW as their mole inside Prabhakaran's hitherto impenetrable ranks as early as 1989, one RAW operative, requesting anonymity, tells me. He would become their deep asset, the one who would subvert the insurgent movement from the inside, and had been tasked to eliminate Prabhakaran and take over the LTTE.

He was first noticed by Col Hariharan within months of the IPKF's takeover at the Palaly airbase in 1987 and after the infamous suicide of an LTTE squad of twelve men early in October.

'You tell the colonel that for these twelve dead men, they will have to collect the bodies of 1200 dead Indian soldiers.' This was the parting shot of the newly appointed deputy head of the LTTE, Mahattaya, to Hariharan, when he came to collect the bodies of twelve Tamil Tigers, including those of Pulendran and Kumarappah, who had committed suicide on 5 October 1987. They had consumed the cyanide capsules that Mahattaya had secretly passed on to them.

Five more Tigers who had been detained along with the twelve off Palk Strait by the Sri Lanka Navy would die later that night. All seventeen ingested the capsules that Mahattaya had dispatched to them—in an engineered taking of their own lives—as the captured LTTE squad was being forced to board a flight to Colombo from the Palaly airbase, guarded by Indian and Sri Lankan soldiers.

Mahattaya's outburst was provoked when he arrived in Palaly with Prabhakaran's lawyer, Shankar, to collect the bodies from the Sri Lanka Army and overheard Col Hariharan warning the lawyer, whom he knew personally, against harbouring any thoughts of going to war with India.

The colonel recounts how he told the lawyer to tell 'Thambi' that it would be a bad idea to turn their guns on India, and that they had been fighting the Nagas for forty years and had the power to go on forever. 'You tell Thambi not to do this,' Col Hariharan said. Shankar smiled and said, 'I may agree with you; but who is going to tell Thambi?'

(Thambi stands for younger brother in Tamil and is the moniker, along with Anna, or older brother, that was universally used for Prabhakaran).

This is when Mahattaya, who overheard the conversation, told Shankar to tell Col Hariharan in a not-so-veiled counter-threat, that the Indian army would have to collect 1200 bodies for the twelve dead Tamils.

Mahattaya had earlier been ill-advisedly allowed by the Indian Army to meet the squad, which is when he secretly handed over the cyanide to them. And India, in charge of their security, would be blamed for their deaths.

Col Hariharan recounts how he and a complement of Indian soldiers were forced to 'watch dumbly as the Sri Lankan soldiers even resorted to kicking the dead LTTE cadres'. Protocol dictated they could not interfere.

'I was there, present at the site, and watched as they chewed the cyanide capsules and immediately began frothing at the mouth. They were dying even as they were being loaded into the SLA ambulance,' he said, the frustration of the time still rankling, twenty-eight years after the event.

'We were given strict instructions to do nothing, to lay off,' said the colonel. 'We had provided doctors to the Sri

Lankan military hospital to attend to them.' But that was all India was allowed to do. Making matters worse was the relationship between the GOC Lt Gen. Harkirat Singh and High Commissioner Dixit.

The Indian Army commander, citing military protocol, refused to take instructions from the Indian high commissioner who wanted to stop the Sri Lanka Army from flying the LTTE men out. It was the starting point for an epic fallout between Lt Gen. Singh and Dixit that would ultimately end in the GOC being recalled.

The inability of the two men to see eye-to-eye on tackling the LTTE was a reflection of a long-running turf war between the military and civilian establishments that cast a dark shadow over Indian troop deployment in Sri Lanka. It marred military engagements and complicated matters even further for the duration of the IPKF's deployment in Sri Lanka, and impacted relations between New Delhi and Colombo.

'Nothing's changed, it continues to this day,' said Vice Admiral (Retd) P.J. Jacob, speaking from his office in Bengaluru. As head of the navy's Southern Command, it was Jacob who oversaw LTTE commander Kittu's watery grave. It was an operation which set off another controversy when the LTTE discovered that it was Mahattaya who had tipped off RAW, that had, in turn, alerted the Indian Navy. Kittu was one of RAW's favourites; nurtured over the years, he was said to have been in the pay of the intelligence outfit. As RAW's Chandran confirmed, 'He was our man, he was always our man.'

Col Hariharan who quickly became a well-known face in Jaffna says, however, that MI was 'never fully in the loop', even as they all became larger-than-life targets. Hariharan and his brother, a surgeon who had treated the LTTE commander Kittu in Madras after a bomb attack blew off one of his legs, bore a striking resemblance to each other. The LTTE leaders knew Col Hariharan's name and face, and who and what he stood for. He knew he was a marked man. 'They kept an enlarged photo of me in their bunkers to potentially spot me and, who knows, take a pot shot. They even shot dead my orderly!'

More than anything, the Palaly incident drove home the point that the Indian military, the civilian intelligence and the diplomats worked at cross-purposes, the one not knowing what the other did.

Unlike the Bangladesh war which was planned with the then prime minister, Indira Gandhi, and the military chief working in tandem, the deployment of Indian troops in Sri Lanka was a decision taken by Rajiv Gandhi and a few of his advisers, without the range of consultations with the army, headed by the flamboyant General K. Sundarji, or MI that was the need of the hour.

As Dixit admits in his book *Assignment Colombo*, Rajiv Gandhi had tried to persuade Jayewardene to drop his xenophobic anti-Tamil attacks for nearly four years.

They went through not one but two rounds of talks at Thimpu, Bhutan, but finally decided to override both sides and push the Indo-Sri Lanka accord through and, with the best of intentions, sent Indian troops to enforce the deal.

The IPKF's initial moves against the LTTE were naturally and expectedly disastrous, based as they were on assessments of the ground situation from the political class and from civilian intelligence that were wrong from the very start.

'RAW may have had a number of moles, but in actual terms, VP [Vellupillai Prabhakaran] was an elusive entity and, therefore, not an easy read. He was autocratic, he was unpredictable, he didn't trust anyone,' says the colonel.

'The army was not privy to inputs from either government or civilian intelligence; they were unaware that an Indo-Sri Lanka agreement was even being signed. This is how governments keep the army out of decisions when they go to war,' rued Col Hariharan.

Vice Admiral (Retd) Jacob agrees, adding that the war against China was conducted by a bureaucrat in the ministry of defence. 'It's what happened in 1962; it's what happened in 1965; it's what happened in 1987.'

The colonel adds: 'My friend in RAW who was put in charge of Sri Lanka operations told me that the army chief Gen. K. Sundarji was not consulted before the decision was made by the prime minister to go for the military option. He said the decision to go to war was made by Rajiv Gandhi, who gave direct instructions to the army chief to send troops to Sri Lanka on the advice of his inner circle.'

The truth, of course, depends on whom you are talking to.

~

But that was not the only weak link. In October 1987, to the embarrassment of the entire RAW top brass, their main man in Madras, K.V. Unnikrishnan, was outed as a CIA mole. He had been leaking secrets on India's clandestine funding, arming and training of Lankan Tamil insurgent groups—which the country had never publicly acknowledged—to the US, which in turn, had been sharing it with Colombo.

When he was arrested and interrogated, it was discovered that he had also shared details of funds, the clandestine arms shipments, all the secret hideouts on both coasts and the names of agents and the actual negotiations with the Tamils for over eighteen months. This was at the time that India and Sri Lanka were working on Rajiv Gandhi's brainchild, the Indo-Sri Lanka peace accord. Rajiv Gandhi's emissary P. Chidambaram was continually taken aback when the Sri Lankans seemed to know the exact details of what he had discussed with the Tamil groups well in advance of every round of negotiations.

The Thimpu peace talks had been similarly compromised and were doomed to fail spectacularly, owing to Unnikrishnan's leak of critical Indian strategy and fallback positions to the CIA, which the US then passed on to Colombo.

The US may, in fact, have lured Unnikrishnan into their net long before he was outed. Unnikrishnan, who served in the Colombo mission, had been compromised when the CIA officer set up a honey trap with a Pan Am airhostess for the gullible Indian agent. No details of the arrest or the charges were ever made public as this would have forced India to come clean on the fact that it was supporting and nurturing an insurgent group.

While feeding the Jayewardene government with information, the CIA had India convinced it was on top of the Lankan crisis although it was completely off its game, with RAW unable to persuade the Tamil protégés they had propped up for so long to do their bidding.

Dixit writes in *Assignment Colombo* about the entry into the Colombo theatre of the CIA's US Gen. Vernon Walters in 1983 as the new ambassador to Sri Lanka. He describes Walters as a 'Cold War warrior, a Henry Kissinger wannabe' and 'the subterranean architect of many of the anti-Indian aspects of US policies on matters of India's national security'.

The question is, what prompted Washington to throw a spanner in India's works?

Walters, feeding into the Sri Lankan President's marked antipathy towards the then Indian premier Indira Gandhi—a feeling shared by the US administration—aimed to cut Sri Lanka out of India's sphere of influence by offering Jayewardene arms supplies and intelligence from Israel, as well as British mercenaries and Pakistani military officers, in return for being allowed to maintain a Voice of America broadcasting station in the strategic port of Trincomalee and the facility to snoop on India's strategic assets.

By the following year, Unnikrishnan had handed over the exact locations of the training camps and the US had satellite photographs at the ready.

According to Dixit, Unnikrishnan 'told his interlocutors in New Delhi that if India kept denying the existence of such camps and did not close them down, the US would release the satellite photographs to the media to embarrass the Government of India'.

Mrs Gandhi's assassination in 1984 was perceived by the Tamils as a blow to their cause, and with her successor, Rajiv Gandhi, casting aside the pro–Lankan-Tamil line, India's intelligence agencies lost what little clout they had over the insurgents.

Dixit himself was soon to run headlong into controversy. Just after the Indian Armed Forces touched down on Sri Lankan soil, co-ordination between the army, military intelligence and the high commission, which was hitherto intermittent to non-existent, turned counter-productive.

'The GOC Gen. Harkirat Singh had a chip on his shoulder about even an MI presence in their midst; this was a malady that afflicted most Indian generals in those days because they never understood MI's role and deployment,' Col Hariharan says.

An object lesson in how things could spin out of control without adequate intelligence on the ground was the Jaffna University debacle in October 1987. RAW was fed false information that Prabhakaran was holed out in the Jaffna University football ground, while his cadres lay in wait for the Indian Army. Col Hariharan characterizes the move to nab Prabhakaran—by throwing not one but three different groups of soldiers, infantry and paras to capture him—as a major op failure. 'MI was not even consulted before the ops.'

The worst was yet to come. The arming of Tamil insurgents, which the colonel had learnt of in 1984 but was 'asked to shut up' about, raised its head as the LTTE began to use those arms to eliminate hundreds of India's Tamil protégés, slaughtering LTTE rivals from TELO and EPRLF.

'When I drew the attention of the MI Directorate, I was asked to proffer advice only when asked, and told that in any case, the army was not training Tamil militants,' he said.

But in an indication of how backing one Tamil militant group while going to war with another would backfire and blow up in India's face, the LTTE began to build bridges with the new Premadasa government with one goal—the IPKF's exit from the Wanni.

This was Prabhakaran at his wiliest, the classic feint of pretending to reach out to the Sinhala majority while using that as a cover to eliminate his rivals and, all the while, buying time to build his own state within a state.

~

Pulling the wool over everyone's eyes, the LTTE number two, Mahattaya, held extensive peace talks in Colombo. The Tiger insurgents even signalled they were committed to finding a political solution to the ethnic impasse by forming an LTTE political wing, the People's Front of Liberation Tigers (PFLT) or Makkal Munnani, which Mahattaya was appointed to head.

Prabhakaran, the man who believed violence was the answer to all his problems, justified the move to mend fences with Sri Lanka's UNP by spinning the fiction that after India's betrayal, they would get a 'better deal' from Premadasa and thus save the Tamil people.

In reality, all he wanted was to use Premadasa who shared Prabhakaran's virulent antipathy against 'foreign troops'—read India—to run the IPKF out of the country.

The first benefits accrued pretty quickly—armed with the weapons supplied by Premadasa and the information on Indian troop movements shared by Sri Lankan intelligence, the Tigers effected huge losses in men and material on the Indian Army in the Wanni region.

'We knew VP was in touch with Premadasa, and that Premadasa had operatives of the Sri Lanka Army spying on our ops and passing the information on to the LTTE. I don't know whether NIB [the Sri Lanka intelligence unit, National Intelligence Bureau] was conducting it. In any case they were tapping my phone whenever I went to Colombo. So I knew that they knew,' Col Hariharan says.

~

While the distrust between India and Prabhakaran persisted, a report that appeared in *The Hindu* on 24 July 1989, about two years after the IPKF's arrival on Lankan shores, headlined 'Prabhakaran Reported Killed in a Shootout' was the proverbial red rag to the LTTE bull.

Once again, as with all secret ops, and unbeknownst to the army, MI or any other agency for that matter, an elaborate strategy by RAW to remove Prabhakaran and replace him with Mahattaya had been put in motion by 1989.

The story, planted in the highly respected Indian newspaper, was meant to unnerve the Tamil community and throw the LTTE off balance. What it actually did was to confirm all of Prabhakaran's worst fears. It exposed RAW's hand. It tipped Prabhakaran off on what awaited him, and it made him all the more relentless in his determination to get the IPKF off the island and wreak vengeance on the highest echelons of the Indian government for attempting to eliminate him. It almost certainly planted the first seed of suspicion in his mind about his deputy, Mahattaya, as he wondered whether he was now in RAW's pay. The report said Mahattaya had killed Prabhakaran in a shoot-out, and proclaimed himself the leader of the Tigers in a widely circulated video.

The report said the shoot-out happened as a result of the two men's differences over making a deal with President Premadasa. 'In the last ten days, top political leaders of the Eelam movement have been eliminated violently . . .' the report said, including 'the outstanding moderate political figure, the veteran A. Amirthalingam, his colleague V. Yogeswaran (TULF), and the leader of PLOTE Uma Maheswaran who earlier lost to Prabhakaran in the violent struggle for supremacy in the militant movement.'

It went on to describe how people had gathered to pay homage to posters of Prabhakaran in the village of Ananthaperiyakulam, 20 kilometres from Vavuniya.

The report stated that the shoot-out, which claimed the life of Prabhakaran's lieutenant Kittu, took place in the Vavuniya jungles from where Prabhakaran was driven out before being shot dead.

But, with Kittu and Maheswaran clearly very much alive, it tipped off the Tiger supremo on what RAW had planned for him. He knew he was the target, that this was a bid to take over the Tigers and place them under a new head, his deputy, Mahattaya. Four years later, Mahattaya, along with over 250 men who were loyal to him, would pay the price for RAW's monumental bungling.

Prabhakaran was already deeply suspicious that the March assassination attempt—when a grenade was lobbed at Kittu in the heart of Jaffna city—was the handiwork of either RAW or Mahattaya. Over and above that, Mahattaya's frequent two-way radio chatter with Madras—which was not with the LTTE remnants there—reinforced Prabhakaran's suspicion that the man he had grown to trust was playing a double game.

But it would take the Indian Navy's attempt to commandeer the ship in which Prabhakaran's kinsman and key aide Kittu was attempting to re-enter the north, for Mahattaya's fate to be sealed.

Kittu, crippled, left with only one leg, had been flown to Madras for treatment and was virtually written off as a fighter after that. He ran the LTTE's operations from the Indian city thereon.

Kittu, originally from Velvettithurai like Prabhakaran, and related to him by blood, as were many of the LTTE cadres, made a name for his ruthlessness and the cold-blooded manner in which he pumped twenty-eight bullets into TELO chief Sri Sabaratnam even as he begged for his life.

As one of the war wounded, he could not aspire to rival Mahattaya or, for that matter, Prabhakaran, whom he had reportedly sought to replace in Jaffna when the main LTTE operations were being run by the big chief out of India.

Kittu, entrusted with the LTTE's operations in Madras in 1988, was both canny and ruthless. His brutal kangaroo courts almost always ended with the mass murder of Tamil civilians, whose bodies were 'dumped' in pits serving as mass graves that became common all across the north.

He oversaw the elimination of hundreds of TELO cadres and freely admitted it was not punishment for the alleged extortion of Jaffnaites—as put out by the LTTE propagandists—but for TELO's links to Indian intelligence agencies.

But his hatred of India notwithstanding, sitting in Madras in 1988, where the LTTE still had the backing, both emotional and material, of the political class and many powerful Tamils, Kittu was not completely immune to RAW persuasion either.

Indian counter-intelligence operatives wooed him relentlessly, and the politically savvy Kittu is said to have finally agreed to send an emissary to Prabhakaran to find a way to end the war between the LTTE and the IPKF which had, at any rate, slowly pushed Prabhakaran back into the Wanni.

The emissary, a man named Johnny, flown in secret into the jungles by the Indian Air Force, didn't get far, a RAW insider said. With no idea that there was even a separate, secret, inside peace track between RAW and the LTTE, IPKF soldiers gunned him down as he headed out on a bicycle towards Prabhakaran's hideout. Even Prabhakaran didn't know he was coming. And a war that could have ended a year and a half before it did, raged on.

By October 1989, Kittu—in a special arrangement with the British High Commission and through the good offices of LTTE ideologue Balasingham—was flown to London where he was met on arrival by officials from the Sri Lankan High Commission and ensconced in 52, Tavistock Lane in London. This left the field wide open for Mahattaya, Kittu's rival for Prabhakaran's affections, to live up to his nickname, 'the big man'.

As early as September 1987, a month after the IPKF landed in Jaffna, Prabhakaran dispatched Mahattaya to trap the top leadership of the PLOTE, and shortly thereafter, to eliminate PLOTE vice chief R. Vasudeva and seventy others in cold blood under the guise of inviting them for a meeting in Batticaloa, while simultaneously sending out teams to wipe out leaders of the EPRLF and ENDLF.

Earlier too, it was Mahattaya who had been given the task of handing over the cyanide capsules to the Pulendran-led LTTE squad detained at Palaly that would set the stage for the final break with India over the IPKF.

The same Mahattaya who, on 6 October 1987, killed five Indian soldiers in Kankensanthurai (KKS) with a garland of burning tyres, which finally led Indian army chief Gen. Sundarji to declare open war against the LTTE the next day, thereby ending the myth of 'peace-keeping'.

It was again Mahattaya who, conveying on Prabhakaran's behalf that the LTTE was in favour of peace, signed a fourteen-point agreement on setting up the interim administration for the Northern and Eastern provinces, counter-signed by the First Secretary at the Indian High Commission, Hardeep Puri, in 1990.

It would later come to light that while Mahattaya was in Colombo, he was assiduously cultivated by RAW's Chandran.

This was the same top spook who had earlier closely worked with Prabhakaran when he was in India. In fact, many say he 'babysat' the Tiger chief through the time he was given arms training in Tamil Nadu, when he was under house arrest in Delhi at Ashok Hotel and, again, during the Thimpu talks. The two are said to have shared an excellent rapport.

One of the rare Indians who spoke and understood Sri Lankan Tamil, Chandran admits as much, saying that Prabhakaran never shared his innermost thoughts, but they did spend time together. 'He loved to eat, he was always fat, not your typical leader on the run. But his appetite for violence was phenomenal.'

The July 1989 report in *The Hindu* on Prabhakaran's death enraged the Tiger leader, frustrated as he was at being pushed back by the IPKF into the Wanni.

The move to contain his deputy-turned-rival would begin by chipping away at Mahattaya's larger-than-life image to show he had blood on his hands. The role of the LTTE and Mahattaya in eliminating Amirthalingam and Yogeswaran was splashed all over Tamil newspapers.

Mahattaya was also given charge of the brutal anti-Muslim pogrom in the Eastern Province that would leave scores dead and displace thousands of Muslim families who were forced to live in camps thereafter, as they do even today. The idea of massacring the Tamil-speaking Muslim community may have been planted in Prabhakaran's head by Colombo's canny UNP leader—a friend of India's—the man who wanted to be President, Gamini Dissanayake, as well as his rival, Athulathmudali, seeking to drive a wedge between the Tamils of the north and the east. Until then, no one treated the Hindu Tamil, Muslim Tamil or Christian Tamil as anything but Tamil.

What it was about Mahattaya's movements that aroused the suspicions of the LTTE supremo and his inner coterie remains unclear. Kittu had been the target of a failed assassination attempt when a man shot at him and then threw a grenade into his vehicle while he was in Jaffna city en route to meet his girlfriend. Though he escaped with his life, he lost a leg. A similar method of attack had been employed against Pottu Amman who had had eight assassination attempts against him, but had escaped unhurt each time. The LTTE boss was led to believe by his inner circle that Mahattaya, at the behest of RAW, was behind the attacks.

Reports of Mahattaya's popularity with both Premadasa and the Indians did not endear him to the leadership either, with Prabhakaran remaining committed to violence, not negotiations or talks, as the only viable means to achieve Eelam.

But when Mahattaya, during an IPKF encounter, inexplicably lost Chunnakam, and the entire Jaffna Peninsula was taken over by the Indian soldiers following a secret meeting at a house nearby with persons unknown, Prabhakaran smelt a rat. The shocking loss of the Eastern Province thereafter to the Sri Lanka Army in 1992, when ties with Colombo predictably unravelled—Colombo had regained control of much of the east and didn't need Prabhakaran—rattled the LTTE leadership and demoralized the rank and file. Mahattaya, accused of poor combat tactics, was summarily relieved of his military responsibilities.

But it would be another three years after the IPKF's exit from the Sri Lankan theatre of war—during which time Mahattaya was effectively sidelined and his rival, 'Baby' Subramaniam, rose to take his place as number two—before the RAW agent's run would come to an end.

Setting the seal on Mahattaya's gory end was the Indian Navy's dramatic capture in January 1993 of a Malaysian-registered ship, the *M.V. Ahat*, that had Kittu on board. To evade capture, Kittu blew himself up along with the ship. The LTTE soon learnt that the man who had tipped off RAW about Kittu's secret presence on the ship that had entered Indian waters and led to his death at sea, was none other than Mahattaya.

Vice Admiral (Retd) Jacob, then commander of the Eastern Fleet, recounts how the Indian Coast Guard's surveillance aircraft, a Dornier, picked out a suspicious ship packed with arms and explosives and tons of fuel—tracked all the way from international waters—as it entered the Indian Exclusive Economic Zone on 6 January 1993, without switching on its lights. The *M.V. Ahat* was in Indian waters.

They had been tipped off by 'actionable intelligence' from RAW, Jacob said. The LTTE, which had been monitoring Mahattaya's radio chatter, learnt that he was the one who tipped off RAW which in turn confirmed to Indian authorities that Kittu had boarded the ship in Singapore. They also confirmed that the ship was packed with arms and explosives for the LTTE that had been procured from Pakistan. Kittu had been expelled from the UK for 'unlawful activities' and met a similar fate when he stayed in France and later in Switzerland, until he surfaced in Singapore, kitted out with a new artificial leg.

There was little doubt that Mahattaya wanted to prevent the return of an old rival. As a creature of RAW, it tied into what he was being paid to do.

~

The *M.V. Ahat*, originally the *M.V. Yahata*, which the LTTE had painted over, was registered to Honduras. It had set sail from Phuket, Thailand, and had already been marked out by Indian surveillance.

Shadowed for behaving suspiciously, for frequently changing course, it was asked for its call sign as it entered Indian waters. As the vice admiral said, the Indian Navy knew they had them when they gave out the wrong call sign. After being shadowed for three days, it was finally intercepted and escorted by two Coast Guard vessels, the *CGS Vivek* and the *INS Kirpan*, a missile corvette, towards Madras by the Indian Navy on 13 January.

As it approached Madras, some 700 kilometres from the coast, the crew abandoned the ship and Kittu and eight other LTTE cadres blew themselves up.

The vice admiral says he remembers ordering the blown-up ship to be boarded and every man on it to be taken into custody. 'The smuggling of arms and weapons by the LTTE had grown. Our seas were infested with small boats and big boats carrying arms and ammo for the LTTE. The Sri Lanka Navy and the Indian Navy worked together very closely on this. Contrary to what is believed, it's India that in recent years has supplied them with fast-speed attack boats and a newly refitted frigate,' said the vice admiral who would go on to become India's deputy National Security Adviser.

A couple of months later, after a public sharing of the charge sheet by an LTTE kangaroo court, a team of top LTTE commanders led by Pottu Amman and including the head of an elite hit squad and the naval chief of the LTTE's Sea Tigers, Cdr Soosai, arrived at Mahattaya's home base in Manipay on 31 March 1993. Reports say Mahattaya was taken to the LTTE camp in Chavakachcheri and tortured over a period of several weeks and months until he could barely speak, sit or stand. He was finally executed in December 1994, nineteen months after he was led away from his home. Some 257 of his men were executed and their bodies dumped, LTTE-style, in a pit and set on fire.

In fact, Mahattaya's and RAW's plan to bump off Prabhakaran had come unstuck several times before. The first was when Mahattaya's close aide, a man called Suresh, was unable to get the message in time to a hitman, Susilan, whom he had planted in Prabhakaran's security detail. Suresh, who only got as far as Putur, was caught by the LTTE intelligence unit.

The second time, another LTTE activist based in Madras, a wounded one-legged operative named Engineer, was spotted in Jaffna by Pottu Amman and taken into custody. Engineer spilled the beans on the RAW plan to take over the LTTE by bringing Mahattaya out from the cold, eliminating Prabhakaran and installing the 'big man' in his place. Engineer had been approached by RAW after hundreds of LTTE cadres living in Madras had been picked up for questioning after the assassination of Rajiv Gandhi. The Indian operatives persuaded him to go to Mahattaya and inform him to put the 'Assassinate VP' plan in action. Mahattaya, in turn, sent Suresh to get the hitman, Susilan, in Prabhakaran's security detail to shoot the LTTE leader.

The third and most serious attempt to eliminate Prabhakaran was when Mahattaya used a back-up hit team of fourteen LTTE prisoners to kill him by planting a bomb in his sleeping quarters. The fourteen homecoming heroes were sent speedboats by the LTTE and were on their way to Jaffna after a purported jail break from Vellore jail! If it hadn't been for a tip-off from an insider, the story of the LTTE may have ended there. The fourteen, detained by the LTTE intel unit, revealed the entire plan to their interrogators.

Adele, wife of former party ideologue Anton Balasingham, in her book *The Will to Freedom*[2] writes:

> Mahathaya and some of his close associates were
> arrested by the LTTE's intelligence wing for conspiring

---

[2] Adele Balasingham, *The Will to Freedom: An Inside View of Tamil Resistance* (Mitcham: Fairmax Publishing, 2003).

to assassinate Mr Pirabakaran. In a massive cordon and search of his camp in Manipay—supervised by senior commanders of the LTTE—Mahattaya was taken into custody along with his friends. We were shocked and surprised by this sudden turn of events. Mr Pirabakaran, who visited our residence that day, told us briefly of a plot hatched by the Indian external intelligence agency—the RAW—involving Mahattaya as the chief conspirator to assassinate him and to take over the leadership of the LTTE. He also said that further investigations were needed to unravel the full scope of the conspiracy.

Mahattaya. The RAW mole that didn't get away. Both a victim and an example of Indian intel's bungling.

6

White Vans, White Flags

'A FEW HOURS AGO ON Tuesday morning [19 May], our ground troops confirmed that they have recovered the dead body of the world's most ruthless terrorist leader. I make this disclosure with responsibility and pleasure as millions of Sri Lankans as well as the army would be most delighted at this news.'

—*Sri Lanka Army Chief Lt Gen. Sarath Fonseka*

At 12.30 p.m. on 19 May, Gen. Fonseka exulted in the gory end of Prabhakaran, the leader of the LTTE, the man who had the blood of Indian Prime Minister Rajiv Gandhi on his hands, and that of countless others, Tamil and Sinhala.

~

On a sweltering day in October 2015, the guards at the spanking new army checkpoint at Vaduvakkal bridge paid little heed as our bright yellow Nano slowed and we took in the sight of the lone fisherman standing in the shallows, casting his net as he perched precariously on the scorched remnants of the bund that had once connected the two sides of the stunningly picturesque waterway.

A stone plaque nearby reads: 'Waduwakkal (sic) causeway is and (sic) important segment which connects Mullaithivu and Pudukuduiruppu. Part of this had been destroyed by terrorist (sic) during the humanitarian operation to prevent advancing (sic) army towards Pudukuduiruppu. The area symbolizes the end of the 14 km long terrorist ditch cum bund which annexed (sic) the No Fire Zone (NFZ) from the rest of the area. The ruthless terrorist (sic) were adamant of holding the innocent civilians in the NFZ . . .'

It is the only sign, bad grammar notwithstanding, that this was the crossing where, on 16 May 2009, death rained down on thousands of Sri Lankan Tamil civilians trapped in the waterway on the last day of the final war against the Tigers led by their brutal leader, Prabhakaran.

Apart from the deeply disturbing documentary *Killing Fields* by the UK's Channel 4, there are dozens of photographs and videos that record the panicked populace picking their way across the bund in a single file— men, women and children—non-combatants alongside belligerents in mufti, their meagre possessions piled on their heads, as they crossed this very waterbody to the so-called No Fire Zone.

Frantically sending text messages on their phones, the LTTE's second rung was reaching out to contacts abroad, from India's Tamil politicians in Chennai to United Nations (UN) officials in New York and former UN peace interlocutors in Oslo with one single purpose—to negotiate safe passage out of the war zone.

The LTTE militia had, in early April, turned thousands of civilians into human shields. But responding to the Sri Lanka Army urging them on megaphones to surrender, many would die when they did just that, mowed down in the crossfire, drowning in the knee-deep waters, their bodies trapped in the rocks below, their possessions, bags and clothing strewn across the blue waters, the white foam awash with their blood. The ones who survived the shelling died a thousand deaths after the battle. They were beaten, raped, taken away and shot dead in horrific acts of vengeance.

The Vaduvakkal death trap. Over 40,000 dead, said the UN Report of the Secretary-General's Panel of Experts on Accountability in Sri Lanka. 'Tens of thousands lost their lives from January to May 2009, many of whom died anonymously in the carnage of the last few days,' the document known as the Darusman Report states. Unofficial figures put the toll at 1,00,000. Official figures would later bring that down to a mere 15,000. Somewhere in between those figures lies the truth.

My companion that October day, Ramkumar, a young journalist from the Tamil newspaper *Virakesari*, cautioned me against taking photos too openly although other war tourists had slowed their vehicles in front of us, clicking pictures as they negotiated the brand-new, narrow bridge that reconnected both sides of the infamous waterway.

It had been six years since the event, and the young man, tellingly, was still worried about attracting undue attention.

Ever since the dramatic setback in the Wanni, as the war came to a head in April 2009, the LTTE forcibly drew the Tamil populace out of their houses, moving thousands to makeshift homes, placing them in tented cities in and around the insurgents' bunkers in Mullaithivu in the hope that it would deter the Sri Lanka Army from attacking them.

As the army closed in, senior members of the LTTE who had concluded they couldn't win the war began actively seeking surrender. From 10 May right up to 16 May, the senior leaders told the trapped civilians in the camps that they were free to go where they pleased, leaving the once tightly monitored checkpoints unmanned.

In a parallel effort to safeguard the civilians, UN peace negotiator Solheim had suggested to the Rajapaksa government that the international community, particularly the US and India, were willing to escort the innocent civilians and LTTE cadres who wanted to surrender to the safe zones.

The plan was to send a ship to the north and the east with UN officials as well as representatives of the international community on board, who would conduct a census, photograph and document all Tamils, divest them of their arms, take them to Colombo and release them later.

Solheim and the LTTE middleman KP were set to meet in Oslo to work out the details on 16 May. Unbeknownst to the thousands waiting in the Wanni, the meeting was called off at the very last moment by Prabhakaran. The suggestion had fallen on deaf ears. President Rajapaksa, visiting Jordan at the time, wanted the LTTE top leadership to surrender to him, and had little intention of letting hundreds of thousands of LTTE sympathizers walk free.

KP would later tell the media that the LTTE leadership was holding out for a conditional surrender that would see the Tiger leadership lay down their arms to a third party, not the Sri Lankan government, in return for a ceasefire and 'negotiations for a political solution'.

Neither the international community—nor Colombo—would have any of it. Nor, for that matter, would Prabhakaran, who had secretly reached out to Delhi through an intermediary to negotiate a separate getaway. Colombo, like the LTTE supremo himself, had other plans.

With Prabhakaran, or someone equally ill-advised, deciding to dispatch two suicide bombers when the mass exodus actually began on the morning of 16 May, hundreds needlessly perished in the fierce do-or-die battle, a journalist embedded with the Sri Lanka Army told me.

All those who wanted to surrender thereafter were looked at with even more suspicion by the Sri Lanka Army. They were asked to strip down, remove their outer clothing, divest themselves of all their possessions, and then come across the water carrying white flags. But it was a charade, a sham, a travesty.

For the army, every Tamil who had lived under the LTTE was suspect, seen as a closet Tiger sympathizer. The men, women and children connected in some way or another to Tiger cadres were, in their eyes, legitimate targets. No one batted an eyelid as the Tamils of the Wanni were taken into custody after publicly surrendering, only to disappear. The 'take no prisoners' directive was in place. This was the White Flag massacre. A day of infamy. There was no documentation, no paperwork, no record of who had been detained.

As the extremely disturbing videos broadcast by Channel 4 and the photographs in various publications and websites around the world show, young boys, girls barely into their teens, women, men, were simply marched behind the nearest truck. Some were raped, all were executed. The terror that marked their horrific and desperately sad last hours, fear written all over their faces, was the price they paid for being of Tamil origin, and living—willingly or under pain of death—under the boot of the LTTE.

The video of the Tamil television presenter Isaipriya's terrified last moments captured the mindless brutality visited on hapless innocents in the dying moments of that war. Barely able to stand, her legs buckling, clearly pleading for her life after she had been raped, the TV anchor whom the soldiers reportedly mistook for Prabhakaran's daughter, Dwaraka, is shown being dragged away by four Sri Lankan soldiers as a naked man walks alongside. Played on Tamil television stations across the world, the popular young woman's gang rape and murderous end epitomized the senseless bloodlust that consumed the Sri Lanka Army as it ended the Tamils' last grasp at freedom.

As the *Sydney Morning Herald* reported:

> The war ended that day. The bodies of some of those who surrendered were found in the days following, but many were not. It is believed that none of those who surrendered, survived.

In the propaganda war unleashed by both sides, and in the bid to cover up the killing of non-combatants that the UN aid agencies would go on to baldly describe as 'genocide', the Sri Lankan media had reported that in the days prior to the last battle, civilians who had attempted to flee LTTE camps had reportedly been killed and their bodies kept on display to deter others from escaping.

Sri Lankan authorities insist that it is these photographs of people killed by the LTTE that were circulated. They claimed they were being unfairly blamed for the White Flag massacre by LTTE remnants deposing before the UN Human Rights Commission in Geneva.

All through the bloody surrenders, only a handful of his close aides were privy to the whereabouts of the LTTE leader. But as the Sri Lanka Army eliminated the last vestiges of opposition, clearing the mangroves and the lagoons of the militia, the hunt for Prabhakaran, whom the Tamils had blindly trusted to guide them to safety, was stepped up. The Sri Lanka Army's special forces tracked him to various locations. His older son, Charles Antony, twenty-four, died as the army drew him out and killed him. If the son was so close, could the father be far behind?

After several false alarms during clearing operations, Prabhakaran's body was found a day later on 17 May, in the flat marshes of the Nanthikadal lagoon just across the bridge. Lying alongside a handful of dead bodyguards, one side of his head blown off, his forehead riddled with bullets, his body lay muddied, blackened, his genitalia covered with a scrap of black cloth.

Nanthikadal. Not the Dunkirk the Tamil diaspora had built it up to be, but the final reckoning. Unlike Vaduvakkal, he didn't even have an escape route into the sea. But diehard LTTE supporters refuse to believe Prabhakaran died in a hail of Sri Lanka Army bullets in these marshes on the day his body was found. Adding fuel to the speculation that he didn't die there, but was inveigled into surrendering and shot, and his body placed later at Nanthikadal, the army chief Gen. Fonseka waited for another forty-eight hours before making the final announcement of his death.

The general—and the Rajapaksa government—clearly wanted to make doubly sure that the body in question was the LTTE supremo's. It was only after Prabhakaran's body was positively identified by two people—the cagey LTTE official spokesperson Dhaya Master who had escaped and been arrested while fleeing with civilians, and former LTTE Eastern Commander Col Karuna who identified Prabhakaran through his identity tag, 001, and the birthmark on his thigh—that the announcement was made.

Conspiracy theorists among the Tamil diaspora, however, insist that Prabhakaran was captured late on the night of 16 May as he thrashed through the marshes attempting to reach his submarine yard just up the coast. This is where, on the turn off to Puthukkudiyiruppu to the ocean, his Sea Tiger naval chief, Commander Soosai, had created a huge semi-submersible that could be launched from a specially built 70-foot-deep water shipyard. That was to have been his escape route. He had no intention of surrendering or getting caught. He wasn't even wearing his cyanide capsule around his neck, and had only a handful of LTTE bodyguards with him.

The rusting, mangled, 30-foot sub that we saw at the submarine yard is a mere shell, a hull, armour-plated and clearly divided into a forward section, a living area, a storage space for cargo and an engine room. It didn't look at all sea-worthy, but six years earlier, it may have been in better shape. Further down the road, in a veritable war museum to the LTTE that now attracts all manner of visitors, there were four mini-subs and several boats that the Sea Tigers had used for gun- and drug-running. Any one of them could have been Prabhakaran's possible ticket to freedom—if he could have got there.

But hemmed in by the sea, backed into a lagoon and in the face of a relentless assault from an advancing army that could almost taste victory, a trapped Prabhakaran no longer had even the element of surprise left. He had only one obvious route—through the mangroves, where the Sri Lanka Army lay in wait for him to break cover. He simply didn't stand a chance.

Since April 2009, several divisions of the Sri Lanka Army had been pushed into Mullaithivu, as had deep-penetration Special Forces, which steadily cleared the entire northern and north-eastern coastline, bunker to bunker, berm to berm, of every single LTTE base in a three-pronged move to close in on Prabhakaran.

On 19 April, Brig. Prasanna De Silva, heading the 55 Division, blew away almost the entire top rung of LTTE commanders in Pudumathalan. By 21 April, he had cleared the A9 highway as he swept from the west coast steadily into Mannar. In the final stages of the battle, it was Maj. Gen. De Silva (promoted after the LTTE was destroyed) who took charge of the key routes alongside Maj. Gen. Chargie Gallage of the 59 Division and Maj. Gen. Shavendra Silva of the 58 Division.

The LTTE which had, at the height of its power, held sway over 15,000 square kilometres of land across the north and the east, were squeezed into a mere sliver of land—42 square kilometres of marsh and mangrove. Prabhakaran, left with no strategy for a counter-attack or a plan to fight his way out, was trapped in the tiny stretch of land at Mullivayikal with no viable exit plan. The army only had to wait for him to break cover.

Sitting out in the Indian Ocean, with the full knowledge of the Sri Lankan naval forces, was the formidable Indian Navy which was working in tandem with the US Navy, using GPS and other navigational tracking devices to monitor the LTTE chief's every move. Using the impressive resources at its command, the Indian Navy was helping to direct the three-pronged attack by Sri Lankan forces that would force Prabhakaran and the handful of men who had stayed with him into the marshy lagoon, just inland, from where there would be no escape.

The firepower that the Sri Lanka Army unleashed over the next seventy hours was fierce. When it ended and the marshes became deathly quiet, the troops were sent to clear out the dead. It was then that Sgt Muthu Banda found a body that looked like Prabhakaran's.

Six years later, we drove into a former LTTE hideout and training yard, barely a stone's throw from Nanthikadal. Complete with a swimming pool and firing ranges and bunkers, tucked inside the Mullaithivu jungle, this was the Tiger leader's preferred lair. The Sri Lankan soldiers had transformed it into a bustling armed camp. As we walked through, a Sri Lankan soldier who accompanied us, pulled me back to recount in broken English how he was right there when Prabhakaran's body was found in Nanthikadal. He said that he and a group of soldiers dragged the body out of the marshes as soon as their fellow sergeant began to shout that the body was Prabhakaran's.

Refusing to tell me his name as he was still in the army, all that the tall, young soldier would say was that while a sergeant found the body, it was a 'colonel' who identified it. It was a day he will never forget. 'My mind went completely blank; I couldn't think straight,' he said. 'But we all knew that this was it, that twenty-six years of war was over, that the man we had come to kill was dead, and yes, we did celebrate, we screamed, we shouted, we fired our weapons, we pulled at his body, shouting that he was dead. It was over,' he said, smiling as he pointed to the LTTE camp they had taken over, and saying with a quiet and unmistakeable sense of triumph: 'They are gone, we are here.'

RAW sources say that until the very last minute, Prabhakaran was tricked into believing that a surrender was a viable option, and that he would be handed over to a neutral international group and not the Sri Lankan government as Colombo wanted.

As the LTTE began to lay down weapons, and the UN negotiators and journalists embedded with the Sri Lankan forces tried to intervene to get safe passage for the LTTE commanders and their families—and failed— Prabhakaran's own surrender plan was being worked out by his supposed trusted confidant KP who has admitted that he had reassured his old friend he would do his best for him.

Unknown to KP, his conversation with Prabhakaran's aide Velu—Prabhakaran never spoke to anyone on the phone—was being monitored by Defence Secretary Gotabaya Rajapaksa. Alongside the 'take no prisoners' diktat that was issued from the very highest levels of the military, the plan to ensure that Prabhakaran did not make a run for it was, clearly, also in place.

KP would later tell a senior journalist of the *Colombo Telegraph* of his shock when he was brought before Rajapaksa after he landed in Colombo following his arrest in the Malaysian capital, Kuala Lumpur, in August 2009. He also spoke of how the secretary of defence would admit to him that he had been listening in on his conversations with Prabhakaran's aide as they discussed the 'surrender.'

While the conflicting accounts of the LTTE supremo's last moments make many Tamils continue to hold to this day that Prabhakaran surrendered and was then executed, and his body placed in the marshes at Nanthikadal, few believe that their 'Annai' could have given up the fight so easily. He showed no signs of having put up a fight. Tamil websites show he did not have a stitch of clothing on him when his body was found and only a part of his head had been blown off, as if he had been shot at close range, perhaps from a few feet away. Most intriguingly, giving the story some credence is the fact that the official photograph distributed by the armed forces shows him fully clothed.

Prabhakaran's final hours—as much of a mystery as his misdirected life.

The central question remains, however: Why would Prabhakaran believe that India, the US, the UK, the EU and Norway would facilitate a surrender—even an unconditional one—and offer him safe passage?

Perhaps, unschooled in the ways of the world and no longer advised by the sophisticated LTTE ideologue Balasingham, who had died in 2006, he was unaware that the leadership in these countries had lost their trust in him after he had repeatedly thrown peace deals and, finally, the Ceasefire Agreement brokered by the international community in 2002, back in their faces. The world had changed since 9/11 and tolerance for his brand of terror was at an all-time low. The US had gone from sympathetic supporter of the Tamil cause to critic as the Tamil diaspora failed to win over the Obama administration. A formal India-brokered safe passage was mere fantasy, given that the government that came back to power in India that very week was led by Sonia Gandhi, widow of the first and only foreign leader he had assassinated in 1991.

KP, who had been estranged from the LTTE leader since 2003, but who had, some say suspiciously, reconciled with his boss as the LTTE's military fortunes nosedived, was strangely his main interlocutor.

Banking on AIADMK leader Jayalalitha as the one who would find a way out showed equally poor judgement. Whether it was an electoral ploy or a gesture to honour her mentor M.G. Ramachandran's friendship with Prabhakaran, she had openly professed her support for Eelam—and then spectacularly lost the Tamil Nadu parliamentary polls.

The question will always be this: Was Prabhakaran under the mistaken impression that India—in tandem with Norway—would step in and give him a safe haven, overlook his past? Or did LTTE sympathizers and the RAW operatives they dealt with grossly miscalculate how far they could go with such a deal? Was Delhi ever on board?

Fonseka Provocation

The actual move to go on the offensive and finish off the Tigers was set rolling after Prabhakaran's ill-considered assassination attempt on the life of Sri Lanka Army Chief Lt Gen. Fonseka on 25 April 2006.

It was Prabhakaran's signal that he formally rejected the 2002 Ceasefire Agreement that had been forged between him and Sri Lankan Prime Minister Wickremesinghe on the active advice of the LTTE leader's own political adviser Balasingham, whom he subsequently relegated to the sidelines.

While the Sri Lankan intelligentsia roundly criticized the move at the time as Ranil's biggest blunder because it gave de facto legitimacy to a terrorist organization that was one step away from declaring a separate state, many have, in retrospect, come to acknowledge that it could have proven to be Ranil's masterstroke. In fact, it may have been the first nail that was driven into the Tigers' collective coffin.

And this is why. As they travelled freely for the first time to the freewheeling, fun-loving Sinhala-dominated south—and foreign countries such as Indonesia—to take part in the peace negotiations, Tigers like Col Karuna Amman, the LTTE eastern commander in charge of Batticaloa and Amparai, got a taste of the good life. In dropping restrictions on travel within the island, the messianic hold of the militaristic Prabhakaran on Tamils weakened as the LTTE leaders moved from their hitherto harsh, grim existence in the jungles to the cities in the south.

The peace talks in Phuket, Thailand, in 2002 to which Prabhakaran had sent Karuna, were an eye-opener for the LTTE commander, sowing the seeds for his final defection from the ranks of the Tigers in 2004. It is in Thailand that Karuna claims he had his epiphany that 'the conflict can only end through political means.'

He is said to have discovered what every peace interlocutor had found—Prabhakaran was never serious about negotiating a genuine peace. This was true when he made a verbal promise to Rajiv Gandhi back in 1987, to President Premadasa in 1989 whom he would assassinate four years later and to President Chandrika Kumaratunga whom he failed to assassinate in 1999, and finally, to Prime Minister Wickremesinghe, with whom peace talks led to a cessation of hostilities and a formal Ceasefire Agreement in 2002 that Prabhakaran, with his continued provocations, showed he had no intention of honouring.

Karuna's defection—whether because he lost faith in a military solution or discovered the good life—however, would prove costly for the Tigers. It meant the loss of its crucial eastern wing. It was from the ranks of the east that the LTTE chief recruited the human cannon fodder he used against the Sri Lanka Army.

Karuna's role as he spilled Tiger secrets and helped unravel the LTTE fighting machine would be key to the destruction of the militants. As he himself admitted in an interview to the *Washington Post* in February 2009, soon after he was rewarded with a ministry in the Rajapaksa government, 'All the world knows that without me, they couldn't have won the war.' He said he knew all the hideouts, all the tactics. 'And without my manpower', the Tigers were left without an army. 'They lost their grip,' he said.

Karuna's publicly articulated grouse stemmed from the fact that it was his soldiers from the east who were used when the LTTE went to war. The top rung of the LTTE leadership comprised northern Tamils, who protected their own while sacrificing his fellow easterners. The breaking point came when, in 2004, he was supposedly ordered to provide another 1000 fighters after he had already forcibly recruited a battalion of child soldiers. Instead, he announced he was quitting the LTTE.

In another ill-judged move, Karuna—unlike Mahattaya, the key Prabhakaran aide who was preparing to remove him, purportedly at the behest of Indian intelligence, and was executed by an unforgiving chief—was never targeted. Colombo, which kept him secure in a safe house, ensured he couldn't be touched.

In keeping with the LTTE leader's classic doublespeak, proffering peace while making war, Prabhakaran compounded that error of judgement on Karuna by attempting to eliminate hardliner Gen. Fonseka. The army chief was badly injured in the April 2006 attack when the LTTE suicide bomber—a pregnant woman—detonated herself at the army headquarters in Colombo just as he was leaving the building.

When Gen. Fonseka resumed active duty several months later, armed with the backing of the international community which worked towards proscribing the terror outfit in thirty-three countries—India had already banned the LTTE in 1992, a year after Rajiv Gandhi's assassination—he was determined to get even. The end of the LTTE was almost a given.

The failed assassination attempt against Gotabaya Rajapaksa on 1 December 2006 sealed their fate.

The Sri Lanka Army, trained and equipped by Israel, India and the United States, first took Mavil Aru in the critical east in July 2006, followed by Sampur in September.

With the full backing of President Mahinda Rajapaksa and his brother Gotabaya, a former military man himself, the Sri Lanka Army under Gen. Fonseka took complete control of the Eastern Province from the LTTE for the first time in fourteen years.

In January 2007, a key town in Batticaloa district was captured. Six months later, Maj. Gen. Gallage wrested the LTTE-held stronghold of Thoppigala from the Tigers. Both in Sampur and Mavil Aru, the LTTE was sucked into fighting a conventional battle. Prabhakaran erred. He had been drawn into a war where he had moved from the hit-and-run strategy of old to the conventional tactics adopted by traditional armies in the battlefield, over which he had no mastery.

He made one more error. In going to war with the Sri Lankan state, which had been prepared to make concessions to his people, Prabhakaran lost the sympathy of the international community which had helped broker the peace.

From 2007 to 2009, as the Sri Lanka Army steadily closed in on the LTTE, with President Rajapaksa determined to take on the LTTE in the east, the Tigers were hit by Karuna's defection. This closed off the supply chain of ammunition, weaponry and military cadres. The LTTE was unprepared for a full-scale offensive, robbed as it was of its eyes and ears, and its access to intelligence and men, money and arms, as Col Karuna went from being Prabhakaran's man to Gotabaya's.

The Sri Lanka Air Force (SLAF) had, in the interim, been honed into a battle-ready squad, trained by the Indians and the Israelis. In November 2007, the SLAF bombed a bunker, barely a few kilometres from the LTTE capital, Kilinochchi, and killed off S.P. Thamilchelvam, the leader of the LTTE's political wing. Thamilchelvam had been talking on a satellite phone to members of his family and the diaspora for several hours at the so-called Peace Secretariat in Kilinochchi, and had just retired to a bunker, when the SLAF's newly acquired Israeli Kfir fighter aircraft let loose a US bomb. Gotabaya is reported to have said: 'We want to give them the message that we know where they are.'

Curiously, the man who had handed Gotabaya the east was on that very same day arrested in London for travelling on a forged passport. If any reinforcement of the theory that it was Karuna who had in fact gifted the east on a platter to the Sri Lanka Army was necessary, it came with his claim that he was travelling on a diplomatic passport arranged for him by Gotabaya. After a nine-month incarceration, he was deported back to Sri Lanka. No charge.

Towards the end of 2008, the Sri Lanka Army finally took control of the LTTE's entire eastern wing, including Batticaloa and Trincomalee, that it had battled to conquer for years.

With that, the separatists lost a vital and strategic artery that connected the eastern waterbody to the northern Wanni hinterland. As India stepped up its vigil in international waters in the north and its navy hindered the once rampant smuggling of weapons and drugs, the LTTE found itself hemmed in from the east as well as the north. The LTTE's fleet of speedboats could no longer bring in arms and equipment or even cash from Malaysia, once arranged through KP, the outfit's arms, cash and drugs procurer.

On 1 January 2009, the LTTE suffered the first of several fatal blows. As the Sri Lanka Army advanced on three fronts, the LTTE lost control of the A9 arterial road from Jaffna. It lost Pooneryn; it lost the strategic Elephant Pass and, within hours, the SLA had overrun the Tigers' administrative capital, Kilinochchi.

Journalists flown in to see the fallen capital recount how every single office in the Peace Secretariat where the LTTE grandees had held court was empty—the offices left wide open with the locks on filing cabinets and storerooms still intact. It was a mine of information on LTTE contacts and their sources of funding overseas. The only thing the LTTE destroyed as they exited was the huge water tank in Kilinochchi, which the Sri Lanka Army has left untouched. Six years later, it's the only remaining symbol of the LTTE's scorched earth policy.

The LTTE abandoned Kilinochchi in great haste. Some 3,00,000 people—cadres and their families, and the farmhands and fisherfolk who worked the land and the sea—were forced to go with them as they retreated deeper and deeper into the Wanni until they were squeezed by government forces into Mullaithivu, the north-east corner of the isle on a strip of land that measured 42 square kilometres.

Trapped or Surrender

The ruthless separatist war waged by the LTTE against the Sinhalese-majority Sri Lankan government came to a bloody end on a desolate beach at Mullaithivu after more than a quarter of a century, in May 2009, when the man who had held out the dream of a separate Tamil state, Ilankai Eelam, was finally snared.

His military might was exposed as nothing more than a myth. Trapped between his own lies and those peddled by the Tamil diaspora, he believed that he was still of some value to the international community. But with no army, territory or a capital, and with a group within his own organization led, many say, by KP, ready to trade him in, in return for their own freedom, Prabhakaran had no cards left to play.

Why he waited for six months from the fall of Kilinochchi in January 2009 to make his strangely addled moves to escape from Mullaithivu makes little sense.

Did he hope to hide among his cadres and take advantage of the assurances of a safe surrender given by President Rajapaksa and his brother, Defence Secretary Gotabaya, to make good his own escape? Was he led to believe that in the last moments of the war, he would be flown out of Mullivayikal to safety by the Indian Navy, only to be betrayed by Delhi working in cahoots with Colombo and Washington?

Did India have the last laugh?

Or does the real story lie somewhere in between—that behind the scenes, Indian spooks with ties to the Tigers had tried to get Prabhakaran and his family to safety, and to help provide safe passage for non-combatants, but failed in the face of Colombo's determination to end the Tamil insurgency once and for all. As a top intel operative told me: 'We stopped trying once we heard of the killing of Balachandran, VP's fourteen-year-old son.' There was no way back after that.

7

The Trial and the Conspiracies

THERE WAS DEATHLY SILENCE IN the Poonamallee courtroom in Chennai as Justice V. Navaneetham walked into the Designated Trial Court on 28 January 1998 and, without further ado, pronounced the death sentence on all twenty-six accused in the Rajiv Gandhi assassination case.

Justice Navaneetham had just made judicial history.

In symbolically breaking the nib of his pen after signing the landmark judgment, he brought to a close one of the longest running trials in Indian history. The trial had passed the death sentence on the largest number of people in any court case in the country and was dubbed a 'judicial massacre' by members of the legal fraternity. The trial had begun on 19 January 1994, two years after Kaarthikeyan, who led the SIT, submitted a formal charge sheet on 22 May 1992 against forty-one people. The specially constituted Terrorist and Disruptive Activities (Prevention) Act (TADA) court-concluded hearings on 5 November 1997, had finally come to an end.

This was closure for the Gandhi family; for the entire nation.

But did it go far enough? Did it lay out clearly how the LTTE managed to catch India's security establishment so completely off guard?

Despite the indictment of governments, politicians and the police by not one but two commissions of inquiry—one headed by Justice J.S. Verma was constituted a week after Rajiv Gandhi's assassination in May 1991 to probe the security lapses; the second, led by Justice Milap Chand Jain and set up on 23 August 1992, was to look into the circumstances of the assassination and the conspiracy angle—the indictments remained on paper.

The Justice Verma Commission described the withdrawal of SPG cover for Rajiv Gandhi as 'unjustified'. It blamed the IB for not keeping Tamil Nadu Police informed of the high threat perception, and the Tamil Nadu police for being unable to prevent the suicide bomber from getting access to the former premier.

The Jain Commission of Inquiry set off a furore in August 1997 when its interim report was leaked, three months before the Designated Trial Court's Judge Navaneetham pronounced his judgment based on the SIT's findings. The Jain report asked why the SIT had not sufficiently probed the nexus between the DMK and the LTTE; it brought up the role played by the godman Chandraswami, and implied that Israeli and US intelligence—Mossad and the CIA—had a hand in Rajiv Gandhi's assassination.

Two of the main accused, LTTE leader Prabhakaran and intelligence chief Pottu Amman, were never extradited. Insiders told me that President Premadasa had communicated to Indian officials it would be difficult to deliver the extradition papers to the LTTE lair in the north as no one dared to enter Tiger territory!

No government in Delhi has pushed for extradition. The LTTE supremo died in a hail of bullets when he was hunted down to the marshy lagoons of Nanthikadal in May 2009. His arms procurer-in-chief—the man who delivered the parts of the belt-bomb to Rajiv Gandhi's assassins in Madras—KP, continues to be at large.

Delhi has not once asked for KP's extradition, with Colombo—and the Narendra Modi government, as strangely silent as the preceding one under Manmohan Singh—being protective of the man who, many believe, was the key to luring the Tiger out of his lair.

While the Sri Lankan government threw up its hands and said there was no way it could bring 'Pirabaharan', nothing was done to bring the other two main accused, his intelligence chief, Pottu Amman, and Akila, the deputy chief of the female wing 'Black Tigresses', to trial either.

No one was prosecuted; nobody was incarcerated except the seven accused.

Was there an attempt to ensure that the blame was laid only at the LTTE's door; and that too, only at the door of these seven? Were the investigators, all of them crack policemen who went by the facts before them, unable to see the big picture, dismissing the dozens of conspiracy theories that were floated—admittedly, most of it conjecture—backed by little or no proof?

Kaarthikeyan, when asked about the differing conclusions he and Justice Jain had drawn, had this to say to his interviewer: 'If you feel that the LTTE would have done this at the behest of anyone else, if you think that the LTTE would have done this for money, then you do not know or understand the Liberation Tigers of Tamil Eelam . . .'

~

The trial itself had been rigorously conducted. In the mind-numbing three years that the sole surviving assassin, Nalini, and her co-conspirators faced judicial scrutiny, the court heard the testimony of 1044 witnesses, of whom 288 were examined. The court also went through 1477 documents presented by the prosecution that ran into 10,000 pages and examined some 1180 pieces of evidence. The defence presented seventy-four documents.

Held in camera, with only two reporters from the official government news agencies present to cover the proceedings, the final judgment held the accused guilty of the charges of conspiracy, as well as offences under the provisions of TADA, the Explosive Substances Act, the Arms Act, the Passport Act, the Foreigners Act and the Wireless and Telegraphy Act, and also under various other sections of the Indian Penal Code (IPC).

Kaarthikeyan said he felt vindicated, that he had been proved right. 'Justice has been served, truth has triumphed,' he told the press as he came out of court that day. 'The nation's and the SIT's single-minded pursuit of truth stand[s] vindicated,' Kaarthikeyan said. 'The court has upheld the SIT's findings and it has been proved that the Indian police are second to none.'

Kaarthikeyan's satisfaction at a job well done came through when he told *Frontline* magazine in May 1992, soon after submitting the charge sheet: 'In the first seven days after the assassination, the world media speculated whether the crime would remain a mystery forever. But, within 10 days we found some slender clues. Within 20 days we made the first arrests—of Bhagyanathan and Padma. We unearthed substantial evidence in 60 days, we made a number of arrests. Within 90 days, we tracked down the main conspirators in Bangalore. The charge-sheet was filed soon after.'

Judge Navaneetham's verdict was in consonance with the findings of Kaarthikeyan's SIT, which was evident from what he would say while delivering the final judgment.

'In this case, Rajiv Gandhi, former Prime Minister, was assassinated in pursuance of a diabolical plot, carefully conceived and executed by a highly organized foreign terrorist organization, the LTTE. Sixteen innocent lives were lost and many sustained grievous/simple injuries . . .' Judge Navaneetham said.

'Considering the above circumstances, I hold this rarest of rare case and I award the death sentence for (sic) the accused,' pronounced Judge Navaneetham, adding that 'from the evidence, oral and documentary, it was established by the prosecution that the conspiracy was hatched by Prabakaran, the LTTE leader.'

The charge sheet filed by the SIT on 22 May 1992 detailed the events that led to the assassination from July 1987 when the IPKF landed in Jaffna, Sri Lanka. It listed forty-one accused.

Of the forty-one, twelve had died—ten of them were Sri Lankans, with three declared proclaimed absconders. None of the final twenty-six accused who were given the death sentence and were in custody, were given bail. All were lodged in the high-security Poonamallee jail.

The accused who were dead included Dhanu, the suicide bomber; 'One-Eyed Jack' alias Sivaresan alias Pakiachandran; Subha, the alternate bomber; the photographer Haribabu; Nehru, the radio operator; and the smuggler Shanmugham. Also dead were the other accused, the LTTE operatives implicated in the plot, Gundu

Santhan, Suresh Master, Dixon alias Kishore, Amman alias Gaigaikumar, Anna alias Kirthi and Kamuna alias Jamila.

The LTTE's supremo Prabhakaran, intelligence chief Pottu Amman and the women's wing deputy chief Akila were the sole surviving Sri Lankan accused. They were declared proclaimed absconders.

The judge announced that the charge of conspiracy had been proved against all the accused, including the thirteen Indians involved.

Reading out the judgment through the day, and that too only the parts that he deemed relevant, the judge stated that the charges against Nalini, Accused No. 1, and Perarivalan, Accused No. 18, under IPC Section 302, had also been proved.

The judge held that Nalini 'shared the common intention to assassinate Rajiv Gandhi' and convicted her under all sixteen counts. The list of charges was exhaustive: Nalini, Accused No. 1, who married Accused No. 3, Murugan, while they were in custody, was charged guilty under Section 3(2) of the TADA as the assassination was a terrorist act committed on Indian soil, under Section 326 of the IPC for causing grievous injuries to thirteen people and under Section 324 for causing simple injuries to six people; she was also found guilty of harbouring, conspiring, abetment and being preparatory to the commissioning of a terrorist act and of indulging in a disruptive act under Section 4(3) of the TADA.

Santhan, Accused No. 2, was found guilty under Section 3(3) of the TADA and Section 14 of the Foreigners Act.

Murugan, Accused No. 3, was found guilty under Section 3(3) of the TADA, Section 14 of the Foreigners Act and Section 6(1) A of the Wireless and Telegraphy Act.

Sankar alias Koneswaran, Accused No. 4; T. Vijayanandan, Accused No. 5; Ruban alias Sureshkumar, Accused No. 6 were found guilty under Section 3(3) of the TADA and Section 14 of the Foreigners Act.

Kanakasabapathy, Accused No. 7, was found guilty under Section 3(3) and 3(4) of the TADA, IPC Section 212 and Section 14 of the Foreigners Act.

Athirai alias Chandralekha, Accused No. 8, was found guilty under Section 3(4) of the TADA, IPC Section 212 and Section 14 of the Foreigners Act.

Perarivalan, Accused No. 18, alleged to have prepared the belt-bomb, was found guilty under Section 3(3) of TADA, Section 302 of the IPC read with Section 109 of the IPC (abetment), Sections 326 and 324 of the IPC. Sections 6(1)A of the Wireless and Telegraphy Act, Section 12 of the Passport Act and Section 4(3) read with Section 4(1) of the TADA. The charge against Perarivalan was that he purchased two 9-volt battery cells to detonate the bomb.

The others convicted were Robert Payas, Accused No. 9; Jayakumar, Accused No. 10; J. Shanthi, Accused

No. 11; P. Vijayan, Accused No. 12; Selvalakshmi, Accused No. 13; Bhaskaran, Accused No. 14; Shanmugavadivelu alias Thambi Anna, Accused No. 15; Ravichandran alias Ravi alias Prakasam, Accused No. 16; Mahesh alias Surendran, Accused No. 17; Irumborai, Accused No. 19; S. Bhagyanathan, Accused No. 20; S. Padma, Accused No. 21; Sundaram alias Subha Sundaram, Accused No. 22; K. Dhanasekaran, Rangan, Accused No. 23; Rangan, Accused No. 24; Vickey alias Vigneswaran, Accused No. 25; and J. Ranganath, Accused No. 26.

Judge Navaneetham's statement in court drew on the evidence that showed 'how the hatred that had been sown in the mind of the LTTE supremo Velupillai Prabakaran, developed into a motive to kill Rajiv Gandhi'.

The judge said Prabhakaran had been 'disappointed' during his visit to Delhi, before the signing of the Indo-Sri Lanka peace accord, when he found that leaders of the other Tamil groups EPRLF, ENDLF, TELO, PLOTE, EROS and TULF had also taken part in the meeting with Rajiv Gandhi in the Indian capital, and that not only was the LTTE not recognized as the sole representative of the Lankan Tamils, it was also not a signatory to the accord.

The judge did bring up the role of Tamil politician Vaiko, a former Rajya Sabha MP and, at the time, a member of the DMK, who would go on to head the breakaway Marumalarchi Dravida Munnetra Kazhagam

(MDMK), as it reinforced the judge's conclusions about Prabhakaran's disappointment.

A video that was submitted as an exhibit shows that on 6 February 1989, Vaiko made a clandestine trip to Jaffna, where he met with the LTTE chief in the jungles of Vavuniya. The prosecution had submitted that in 1988 Vaiko had told the International Tamil Conference in London that Prabhakaran had spoken to him from Delhi on 29 July 1987, where he was kept isolated, with no access to visitors. Prabhakaran would say to him that he had been 'betrayed' by the Government of India and that he had been 'stabbed in the back by Rajiv Gandhi'.

When Vaiko was cross-examined in court, he denied having said any of those things, but the judge concluded that the politician's denial was false, adding that even though the witness had turned hostile, 'his evidence . . . had to be accepted.'

'It was at that point that the seed of hatred against Rajiv Gandhi was sown in the mind of Prabakaran,' said the judge, noting that, 'this hatred gradually developed into animosity against Rajiv Gandhi, in view of the events that took place after the IPKF was inducted in Sri Lanka.'

The judge also pointed to the Congress party manifesto—which spelt out Rajiv Gandhi's commitment to the July 1987 Indo-Sri Lanka accord and his desire to protect the territorial integrity of Sri Lanka, which ran contrary to Prabhakaran's goal of vivisecting the island nation and carving out a homeland for the Tamils—as having contributed to the motive behind the conspiracy. The only way to prevent the Indian leader's return to power was to eliminate him.

Interestingly, referring to the arguments of the defence that many other militant groups such as the ULFA, Jammu and Kashmir militants and Punjab militants were against Rajiv Gandhi, Judge Navaneetham said that 'while it was true that the Indian leader had been at the receiving end of threats from several militant groups in India, there was not an iota of evidence available to support the contention that any other foreign elements were involved'.

'On the other hand, the facts and circumstances have proved, through witnesses and documents, and clearly established beyond any doubt that, Prabakaran and the LTTE alone had a very strong motive to kill Rajiv Gandhi', the judge said, running contrary to the Jain Commission findings which centred on the involvement of 'foreign elements'.

~

Death, Life, Freedom

In February 1998, the defence went in appeal to the Supreme Court against the convictions and the sentences.

But on 11 May 1999, the Supreme Court upheld the death sentence against four of the twenty-six accused, in a 2-1 majority verdict—Nalini; her husband, Murugan; Santhan; and Perarivalan—while commuting the death sentence against three of the accused, Robert Payas, Jayakumar and Ravichandran, to life imprisonment, and acquitting the nineteen others, all of whom walked free.

The bench comprised Justices K.T. Thomas, D.P. Wadhwa and S.S.M. Quadri, and each pronounced a separate verdict, with the last two constituting the majority view. While Justice Thomas and Justice Quadri agreed on awarding the death sentence to three of the accused, there was no agreement on the sentence to Nalini.

Justice Thomas said, 'Nalini was an educated woman' and 'was an obedient participant in the conspiracy, but played no dominant role'. The judge said, 'She was brainwashed by Murugan and others to believe the horrific stories about IPKF excesses in Sri Lanka,' and had told her brother, Bhagyanathan, that she never realized how serious the conspiracy was until it was too late for her to withdraw.

Justice Quadri, however, differed. 'If the death sentence is not awarded to Nalini, who was a willing participant in the conspiracy to kill, then justice would be stunted,' he said.

Justice Wadhwa agreed, saying, 'She was mentally prepared by Dhanu, Sivaresan, Murugan and Subha and she voluntarily participated in the dry run at V.P. Singh's function, held a few days earlier.'

Both Justice Wadhwa and Justice Quadri were in agreement on awarding the death sentence to Nalini.

Justice Thomas observed, however, that, 'As Murugan, the father of their child, was awarded the death sentence, the mother [Nalini] should be saved not to make the child an orphan.' Nalini had married Murugan while in prison, and given birth to a girl child in 1992.

Justice Thomas divided the accused into four categories: the hardcore, those who induced others into the conspiracy and played an active role, those who joined the conspiracy, and those who played a passive role. The judge said all the accused belonging to the first category, including Prabhakaran, were never brought to trial, because they were either dead or absconding.

'The seven accused whose conviction is upheld belong to the second category,' the judge ruled.

While upholding the conviction of these seven accused on the charge of conspiracy to murder Rajiv Gandhi under Sections 302 and 120 (B) of the IPC, the judges set aside their conviction under various provisions of the TADA.

The judges acquitted eighteen of the remaining nineteen accused on the charge of conspiracy to murder Rajiv Gandhi. Their conviction for minor offences was upheld, but they were ordered to be released forthwith, as they had already served the necessary period of imprisonment. One of the accused, S. Shanmugavadivelu, was acquitted of all charges.

Senior advocate N. Natarajan, who appeared for Nalini, Murugan, Santhan and Perarivalan, said the four accused would seek presidential mercy. They would also move the Supreme Court to stay the death sentence until the President acted on their mercy petitions, he added.

The four prisoners were lodged in Central Prison, Vellore. Nalini was shut away in the women's wing.

~

The Seven Lifers

In April 2000, barely two years later, Nalini's death sentence was commuted to life imprisonment. Sonia Gandhi, the Congress party chairperson and Rajiv Gandhi's widow, intervened, as did the Tamil Nadu state cabinet, to make a recommendation to the Tamil Nadu governor and publicly plead for clemency.

The public appeal by Sonia was made on the premise that Nalini was now a mother, and both parents could not be sentenced to death as it would leave the child an orphan.

On 19 March 2008, seventeen years after her father was slain by a human bomb, Rajiv and Sonia Gandhi's daughter, Priyanka Gandhi Vadra, arrived at Vellore Jail to lay her own personal ghosts to rest. She was set to meet face-to-face with the woman who was the sole surviving member of the team of LTTE assassins who did away with her father on the night of 21 May 1991 on a blood-soaked field, some 25 kilometres from Chennai.

'I don't believe in anger, hatred and violence,' Priyanka said in her statement. 'And I refuse to allow it to overpower my life.'

It was a private affair, 'a purely personal visit that I undertook completely on my own initiative', Priyanka said in the statement that was released after news of the meeting with Nalini leaked to the Indian press. 'I would be deeply grateful if this could be respected. . . . It was my way of coming to peace with the violence and loss that I have experienced,' she said.

~

In February 2014, the Supreme Court commuted the death sentence of the three men convicted of assassinating Rajiv Gandhi to life in prison, dismissing the government's appeal that the eleven-year delay in deciding their mercy petitions did not entitle them to a pardon.

The mercy petitions of Santhan, Murugan and Perarivalan had been sent to the President, the last stage in the process of appeals, in 2000. While their mercy petitions were rejected eleven years later, their hanging was stayed in 2011 on the orders of Madras High Court. Three years later, they were no longer on death row.

Freedom for these three and the fourth killer, Nalini, and three others has been taken up by the Jayalalitha government in Tamil Nadu and, at every turn, its efforts to free Rajiv Gandhi's killers has been blocked by the apex court.

Indeed, a day after the Supreme Court order, on 19 February 2014, when the state had suo motu ordered the release of all seven life convicts, the Centre rushed to the Supreme Court and stayed their release.

In March 2016, the Tamil Nadu government once again wrote a similar letter to the ministry of home affairs, seeking its opinion on releasing the seven convicts in the Rajiv Gandhi assassination case. The letter said that while the state had already decided to release them, it was necessary to seek the Centre's opinion under Section 435 of the Code of Criminal Procedure. It said that the Tamil Nadu government had received petitions from all seven convicts—Murugan, Santhan, Perarivalan, Jayakumar, Robert Payas, Ravichandran and Nalini—requesting that they be released as they had spent twenty-four years in prison.

The letter also referred to a writ petition filed by Nalini in Madras High Court seeking her release, noting that four of the seven convicts are Sri Lankan nationals.

In April 2016, the Supreme Court once again rejected the proposal of the Tamil Nadu government—with one eye on the upcoming polls in May 2016—to release the seven lifers. The ministry of home affairs told the state that 'since the matter is sub-judice in the Supreme Court, it has no authority to release the prisoners'.

~

It was in the run-up to the court's verdict in 1998, however, that for reasons that remain unclear, the Congress party and the Gandhi family, acting either on bad advice or bad judgement, believed that the SIT and the specially designated court were not moving fast enough, or in the right direction, and supported the Jain Commission's criticism of the SIT's findings. The SIT was hunting down Rajiv Gandhi's killers, bringing them to justice and preparing the case against them that would be tried in the specially Designated Trial Court. To them, the Jain Commission, set up to probe the conspiracies behind the assassination, was seen to be, as the eminent lawyer A.G. Noorani put it, 'obstructive'.

'The Jain Commission came perilously close to wrecking the trial,' Noorani states. 'Sadly, neither the Supreme Court nor the Delhi High Court cared to intervene. The triumph of justice was due entirely to the integrity and independent spirit of Judges S.M. Sidickk and

V. Navaneetham and to the devoted labours of the Special Investigation Team of the Central Bureau of Investigation headed by its Joint Director D.R. Kaarthikeyan, who showed courage and honesty,' says Noorani. High praise indeed.

In August 1997, an interim report by the Jain Commission was leaked, kicking off a huge storm and inviting even stronger criticism that it was an attempt to prolong the life of the commission with fantastical conspiracy theories.

The seventeen-volume, 5000-page report which had the testimony of some 110 witnesses, unequivocally and baldly stated that without the DMK's support for the LTTE, and the 'deep nexus between the Tamils of Sri Lanka and India', the assassination of Rajiv Gandhi would not have been possible. Although, curiously, by the time the final report was released in July 1998, the findings were less sweeping and bore little relation to the interim report that had been leaked.

The interim report had blamed prime ministers V.P. Singh and Chandrashekhar for not having provided enough security for Rajiv Gandhi. It had devoted several pages to the godman Chandraswami, who, Justice Jain believes, was involved in the high-profile assassination. It remains unexplained why Justice Jain submitted a 2000-page-long final report that watered down the charge made in the previous year's leaked interim report against the Tamils, to say that only 'a few Tamils supported the LTTE' although it continued to maintain that the SIT had failed in its investigation as it had not questioned the DMK leader and Tamil Nadu chief minister, M. Karunanidhi, and a minister in his government, Subbulakshmi Jagadeesan, who allegedly provided refuge to one of the accused, Santhan, in her farmhouse in Coimbatore after the assassination.

Buttressing its argument with reports by the Subsidiary Intelligence Bureau, the Jain Commission said that during 1989–91, 'The LTTE had fertile ground in Tamil Nadu during the DMK rule.' It also said that the ministry of home affairs had been kept informed of the 'material and moral support to the LTTE from DMK sympathisers'.

The Jain Commission report, made public seven years after the assassination, said, 'One such message, sent by the Additional Director of the Intelligence Bureau (IB) to the Home Secretary on January 30, 1990 states: "The LTTE has been taking full advantage of the sympathies of the DMK in Tamil Nadu . . . local DMK leaders in the coastal region of Thanjavur have also been collaborating with the LTTE in their illegal trafficking and activities . . ."' It is for this reason that Justice Jain he felt 'the Tamil Nadu Chief Minister, M. Karunanidhi should have been among the politicians, who were questioned by the Special Investigating Team (SIT). On many matters his interrogation was quite relevant.'

In Justice Jain's list of additional suspects were another twenty-one people whom, it said, the SIT should have investigated. Apart from the ten Indians on the list, he named eleven Sri Lankans, including the LTTE's financier and arms buyer Kumaran Pathmanathan, 'KP'; its London-based international spokesperson Col Kittu; 'Baby' Subramaniam; and Muthuraja.

Jain says, contrary to the assertion (during deposition) of SIT chief Kaarthikeyan that there 'is little scope of involvement of any other persons', his conclusion was that the SIT should have filed supplementary charge sheets against a 'large number' of persons.

(The Congress party's agitation, incidentally, that used the Jain Commission interim report against the then DMK government, which was allied with I.K. Gujral's United Front government at the Centre, achieved its immediate aim—toppling the Gujral government—but paved the way for the entry of the Atal Bihari Vajpayee-led BJP government in Delhi.)

Noorani's main criticism rests on the premise that Justice Jain, in pursuing 'the conspiracy theory', was simply grabbing at straws. 'The charge sheet rested squarely on a conspiracy by the LTTE. Independent journalistic investigation supported the charge. International perception did not differ. President Chandrika Kumaratunga publicly blamed the LTTE', he said. Yet, Justice Jain believed there was more to the assassination than the LTTE.

The premise of the two commissions of inquiry differed. As Noorani writes in *Frontline* in February 1998, 'While the Jain Commission, set up on 23 August 1992, had one main remit, the conspiracy aspect, which Justice J.S. Verma had refused to accept . . . Justice Verma confined his inquiry, set up on May 27, 1991, to security failures alone, personal or systemic.' Noorani says Jain was directed to inquire into 'the sequence of events leading to, and all the facts and circumstances relating to the assassination of Mr Rajiv Gandhi at Sriperumbudur (other than the matters covered by the terms of reference for the Commission headed by Justice Verma)'. In particular, Noorani states, the commission was enjoined to inquire 'whether one person or persons or agencies were responsible for conceiving, preparing and planning the assassination and whether there was any conspiracy in this behalf and, if so, all its ramifications'.

'For such an inquiry to declare open season on lurid conspiracy theories was to cast aspersions on the charge sheet,' Noorani added.

The question is—did it?

SIT investigator Ragothaman adds a curious—and troubling—new charge. He says that for the LTTE, this was the perfect scenario as, by law, they could not be charged by two courts, in this case the Designated Trial Court and the Jain Commission of Inquiry findings when they were submitted. If the Jain Commission which was demanding access to all the letters and documents that the SIT had, found one of the LTTE accused not guilty, then the special court could not hold them or charge them.

Ragothaman said that lawyers for the accused, and Murugan and the other LTTE accused, became supremely confident and came to believe that the SIT and the Jain Commission would cancel each other out and they would soon walk free.

In fact, as Noorani explains, a trial and an inquiry can proceed simultaneously. 'But a heavy onus lies on the judge holding the inquiry to ensure that the trial proceedings are neither obstructed, whether by seeking its records or otherwise, nor prejudiced.'

Noorani said that as the head of the panel probing the conspiracy angle of the assassination, Justice M.C. Jain, in announcing that the Jain Commission had decided to form its own investigating team to evaluate the findings of the CBI's SIT in the Rajiv Gandhi case and search for further evidence if necessary, 'threatened the orderly course and integrity of the trial proceedings'.

Jain asked the home ministry to provide him with a particular inspector general in the CBI, fluent in Tamil, for the assignment. 'The IG will go after leads missed by the SIT. The Commission will examine the entire SIT material and verify its correctness,' Justice Jain told the *Indian Express* in 1992. 'Under the IG will be a team of investigating officials. The commission would sit in judgement on the SIT's investigations as well as draw on its labours.

Noorani says this 'brazenly violated the Commissions of Inquiry Act, 1952, and established precedents'. Three years later, in an order made on 28 December 1995 that was in flagrant breach of the Commissions of Inquiry Act, Jain asserted that 'the Commission is entitled to know as to how and in what manner the SIT proceeded with the investigation. It is only after looking into the record—such as the case diary before the Designated Court—that the Commission would be able to know as to what leads have not been investigated and investigation of what leads has not been completed, who are the suspects and what evidence is available against them . . .' In other words, a parallel investigation and a parallel court.

In Poonamallee court jail, the LTTE inmates were certain it would only be a short while before they could all go home.

How far off the mark was Justice Jain on the conspiracy theory?

In a curious contradiction, little known and never reported, is the fascinating story behind the exit of Gopal Subramaniam, who, acting as counsel (in 1991–92) to the judicial commission headed by Justice Verma to inquire into security lapses leading to the assassination, quit

after lawyers close to Sonia Gandhi advised him to steer
clear of conspiracy theories.

~

The haste with which Sivaresan's body was cremated—
under tight security at Bangalore's Wilson Garden
crematorium on 3 September 1991—and the manner of his
death, a bullet to his head rather than cyanide, only fuelled
the cover-up theory. This was made worse when a local
Congress functionary close to the LTTE, Shanmugham,
was found hanging from a tree, while in SIT custody. The
SIT was accused of silencing him.

When weighed in the balance, the Jain Commission
and the SIT headed by Kaarthikeyan correctly deduced
that the assassination was the handiwork of Prabhakaran.
But they failed to squelch speculation, then, as much as
now, that there could be more.

8

The Lost Legacy

WHERE ONCE THERE WERE ONLY the walking wounded, empty streets, grim faces and bombed-out buildings, there is traffic! And it has been brought to a complete standstill in Jaffna this morning as schoolchildren in crisp white-and-blue uniforms march by, led by youthful teachers, yelling out lustily in a celebration of Boy Scouts Day.

The young! In a city that once hid away any young person—man or woman—who could be forcibly recruited by the Tigers.

Eight years of an uneasy peace without the Tiger imprimatur; almost twenty-five years since one of their own had Rajiv Gandhi killed in cold blood. This is a Jaffna, the once notional capital of Tamil Eelam—and India's Vietnam—that is in the throes of a complete makeover.

The cagey, shifty-eyed trishaw drivers in scruffy dhotis, the Tigers' self-appointed secret service, who once owned the main street and openly grilled you—and every newcomer—are long gone.

'You don't look Tamil, how do you know Tamil?' would be the first salvo as they veered off the path to show you the home of LTTE commander Pottu Amman's girlfriend as one driver did when I was there in the late 1990s. More pointedly, once they knew you were an Indian, they would take vicarious pleasure in driving you past Prabhakaran's hideout in Jaffna University from where the LTTE chief's perfectly positioned machine guns had blown the Indian Army's heli-borne troops out of a moonlit sky.

Last but not least, you would be shown the Jaffna native's biggest bugbear, the Buddhist *viharas*, the temples that mark the footprint of the Sri Lankan army—an enduring imprint of Sinhala chauvinism, an old wound that eats away at the Tamil to this day.

The trishaw driver I hire from the surprisingly well-organized taxi rink in October 2015, who takes me to my hotel, so new that even he hasn't heard about it—next to the spanking new railway station that India has rebuilt to reconnect the north to cities in the south—has a whole new target for his gripe. It isn't the Sri Lankan soldiers who have escorted us into the city from the Palaly airbase. Or India. Or Rajiv Gandhi whom most Lankan Tamils, like the current member of the Provincial Council, the highly vocal Ananthi Sasitharan, blame for introducing their young to the culture of violence that wrecked their lives. He reserves his venom for Jaffna's political class that hasn't lived up to its promises.

It's at night that you get a glimpse of the dramatic dawn that is at hand. No longer the ghost city of deserted streets and long shadows that it once was, at sundown, the young, clad in hip T-shirts and jeans take over, whizzing past on motorbikes, doing wheelies on newly tarred roads, past homes that are being reconstructed.

My taxi driver, Rajiv—a fairly common name in these parts—is barely out of his teens and already the owner of a car. He says, without batting an eyelid as he drops me off at 9 p.m., that he will come back for me by midnight, as if this is all par for the course!

At Hotel Tilko's open-air restaurant where I am set to have dinner with Jaffna's large-hearted surgeon Dr Ravi Perumpillai—who moved back from London soon after the Tiger debacle to set up the city's first surgical heart unit here—there is loud music . . . and alcohol. The puritanical ways of the Prabhakaran era were clearly at an end.

The bouncer at Tilko overseeing the youthful exuberance of the post-LTTE era is, in fact, a hulking seven-foot-something former Tamil Tiger. Dr Pillai tells me his new cook-cum-housekeeper once served with the LTTE. 'All my nurses at the hospital are also ex-LTTE. They don't have formal training, which they are getting now, but they have something rarer—on-the-field training,' said the surgeon.

Jaffna Fort, framed in the moonlight, is no longer a Sri Lankan army fortress, but lit up—the Portuguese-built citadel is primed for a transformation into a tourist hub with a makeover on the lines of Galle Fort and Colombo's stunning Independence Memorial hall.

The Jaffna Football Stadium where an all-Lanka football tournament is underway is being speedily renovated under the supervision of the Indian consulate—the only foreign mission here—at a cost of Rs 7.1 crore, ahead of a video inauguration by Indian Prime Minister Narendra Modi in June 2016. It will be named after Duraiappah, the first mayor of Jaffna, who was Prabhakaran's first 'kill'. Until recently, it also held the grisly remains of a mass grave. Few of the Tamil teenagers playing at the stadium now will recall the blood spilled on these very same grounds—by the LTTE and by Rajiv Gandhi's IPKF nearly thirty years ago.

Ever since the guns finally fell silent in 2009, a clutch of doctors such as Dr Pillai, health workers, intellectuals, hoteliers and restaurateurs, even travel agents and corporates, many funded by the Tamil diaspora, have flooded back in and simply transformed the Jaffna of old.

There are reports of the re-emergence of a religious right, a conservative backlash against the growing drug culture and promiscuity, virtually non-existent under Prabhakaran's diktat.

Yet, Jaffna, once so tightly wound, exudes for the first time the flavour of a freewheeling town. No longer the grim, joyless place it once was, Jaffna's most heartening sound today is that of people laughing—out loud.

~

Any regret over the Indian premier's assassination that is trotted out when one steers the conversation in that direction, to remind them that it was Rajiv Gandhi who first came to their rescue, is at best perfunctory, embarrassed.

The assassination was a blunder, yes. And a shock, they say. As the venerable Rajavarothiam Sampanthan, who heads the moderate Tamil National Alliance (TNA) and is the leader of the Opposition in Parliament, emotionally admits, 'We feel an enormous sense of regret and sadness that Rajiv Gandhi was killed by a Tamil suicide bomber. I met him innumerable times, trying to find a way for our people to get their rightful place in Sri Lankan society, and he was always supportive. It was a huge shock. It simply should not have happened.'

But for most others, it was nothing more than one of many deaths in a sea of assassinations that became part of their blood-soaked history.

It has been almost thirty years since the young men in Ananthi's own neighbourhood took up arms, but she reserves her most trenchant criticism for the Indian

leaders who she believes were behind the upheaval—
Indira Gandhi and Rajiv Gandhi.

She says that as a sixteen-year-old, long before the
IPKF was even deployed in the north, she witnessed the
radicalization of young Tamils by the Indians. 'The Sri
Lankan army was rounding up all Tamil youth who were
critical of the government, and yes, the officers targeted
all the young girls, including many like me, coming to our
homes and demanding our presence in their barracks.
Many of us ran away. But the people who put guns in the
hands of our young men, who until then only knew a life
of books and debates, were your leaders. Indira Gandhi
and Rajiv Gandhi. They taught them how to fight, how to
use guns. Before that, we didn't know the first thing about
war. And then Rajiv sent in the Indian Army to fight our
people, when they should have helped us to fight the Sri
Lanka Army. This was the great betrayal. How can we
forgive that?' she asks.

Ananthi's is the prevailing view of Indian involvement
in the Lankan Tamils' battle for survival against the Sri
Lanka Army in the cities of the north that are still living
on the knife-edge of an unlikely peace.

The unpleasant truth—Rajiv's intervention would not
earn him the gratitude of the Jaffnaite, even though he did
so in their name. Today, barely anyone remembers that it
was the siege of their city by the Sri Lanka Army in June
1987 that would be pivotal in the Indian prime minister's

decision to radically shift the goalposts on Sri Lanka and go from neutral interlocutor to Tamil saviour of sorts.

After the bombing of Jaffna, a deliberate provocation by the Jayewardene government, the Indian prime minister initially tried to mediate between the two warring sides. The rules of the game changed when, under Delhi's watchful eye, Colombo—which had been beefing up its armed forces through 1985–86—launched Operation Liberation, sending 4000 Sri Lankan soldiers into Jaffna city, rounding up 3500 young Tamils and bombing LTTE hideouts. As civilians flooded to safe havens across the Palk Strait, there was an outcry in Tamil Nadu. The domestic fallout forced Rajiv Gandhi to rethink his hitherto hands-off policy, as his own Intelligence Bureau warned of a Tamil backlash against the central government's perceived inaction. As attempts at a truce floundered in the face of Jayewardene's continuing crackdown on the LTTE, Rajiv Gandhi led India into the first direct intervention in Sri Lankan affairs.

The Kachchativu standoff lasted for barely four hours on 2 June 1987, until the Sri Lankan navy escorted the flotilla of nineteen unarmed Indian boats loaded with food and medicines for the besieged people of Jaffna out of Sri Lankan waters. The Indian Navy was positioned ominously, barely 30 kilometres away, in international waters. Within forty-eight hours, Rajiv Gandhi would up the ante. After warning the Sri Lankan high commissioner in Delhi—a mere hour before the Indian Air Force (IAF) squadron took off from Yelahanka airbase in Bangalore—of military retaliation if they were thwarted again, he followed up Sri Lanka's naval blockade with Operation Poomalai, a provocative airdrop of supplies over Jaffna by the IAF on 4 June that Colombo prudently chose not to challenge.

A show of force, it was only 25 kg of supplies, airdropped a few miles from Jaffna. It was barely enough to feed a handful of families. But in strategic terms, the Jaffna siege was the closest that India and Sri Lanka came to an all-out war, until the famed standoff in 1990 between Sri Lankan President Premadasa and India's IPKF GOC-in-C, Gen. Kalkat, when India was asked to withdraw its troops or be seen as enemy combatants.

The airdrop was Rajiv Gandhi's signal to the Jayewardene government that the ill treatment of Sri Lankan Tamils—a domestic hot potato—coupled with the bigger issue, challenging India's writ in its own backyard, would come at a price. India, on 4 June 1987, officially charged 'the Government of Sri Lanka with denying the people of Jaffna their basic rights', saying that India could not remain 'indifferent spectators as hundreds of civilians died and many more faced starvation'. Within sixty days, however, despite being the only Indian leader to 'fight' for the rights of the Lankan Tamils by putting Indian boots on the ground, he would earn the implacable hatred of the

Colombo elite and the only Lankan Tamil he left out of the peace deal.

In a city inured to more than thirty years of bloodletting and war, and brought up on a diet of unadulterated Tiger propaganda, it's no surprise that nobody in the Jaffna of today can—or will—recall the events with any clarity beyond the satisfaction that Sri Lanka—and the Tamil Tigers—gave Rajiv Gandhi's India a bloody nose when he shifted gears again, abandoning the LTTE and going back to doing business with Colombo.

~

Rajiv Gandhi, Architect of Devolution

Not many in Sri Lanka's north care to remember that the much-touted devolution of power to the Tamils worked into the Indo-Sri Lanka agreement of July 1987, and once again central to the Tamils' quest for equal rights, was Rajiv Gandhi's brainchild.

First incorporated in the Indo-Sri Lanka Accord signed by Rajiv Gandhi and Jayewardene on 29 July 1987, the 13th Amendment to the Constitution of Sri Lanka was passed on 14 November 1987. The Provincial Councils Act, passed by the Parliament alongside the 13th Amendment, legalized the establishment of provincial councils, the devolution of power to them, and the merger of the Northern and Eastern councils, while declaring Sinhala and Tamil as the national languages and retaining English as the link language.

In fact, Rajiv Gandhi, moved more by reasons of geopolitics than just sympathy for the Sri Lankan Tamils, was the first foreign leader to weigh in on the side of the Tamils after the Sri Lankan government, in 1974, passed laws that the Tamil minority perceived as discriminatory.

The sizeable Tamil minority—roughly 11 per cent of the 20 million Sri Lankans—had begun a peaceful, democratic push for greater autonomy which was deemed unconstitutional through the 6th amendment of the Sri Lankan Constitution in 1983.

The devolution that Rajiv Gandhi backed would become a deeply divisive and contentious issue. It was seen by both the moderates and Sinhala chauvinists as a gross interference in Lankan affairs because it sought to give the Tamil people a status equal to that of the Sinhala majority, and no government in Colombo was willing to fully implement its provisions.

The foot-dragging by the Jayewardene government over implementing the 13th Amendment would alienate the Tamils further. LTTE chief Prabhakaran cleverly tapped into the deep disillusionment of the highly erudite, aspirational Tamil populace with Colombo's continued discrimination to build support for his own violent, secessionist movement.

Support for Prabhakaran was unwavering even when it came to the most dastardly LTTE criminality of all, the forcible recruitment of boys and girls as child soldiers. In the early days, and unlike the other separatists, the group led by Prabhakaran—who projected himself as the saviour, the only leader who could deliver the Tamils from Sinhala duplicity—drew the angry Tamils to them in droves. Many were relatives of Prabhakaran himself and came from in and around the villages of Velvettithurai, his home town.

The draw of the LTTE was such that it attracted both the educated and the uneducated, the tillers as well as the teachers, and hundreds of young people barely out of their teens. At least a third of the Tigers, recruited forcibly or otherwise, comprised young girls and women, with close to 6000 of these female soldiers dying in battle.

But as the LTTE grew into a status quo power that ran a supremely efficient, de facto police state in the north and the east of Sri Lanka, there was a concomitant drop in the numbers gravitating towards the Tiger army. Forcible recruitment became the order of the day, and heading the drive to make up for the shortfall in the Tigers' lower ranks was a flamboyant LTTE commander called Ellilan, who allegedly struck terror in the hearts of ordinary Tamils when he came knocking on their doors, asking for their children.

But say that to the poster girl for the LTTE remnants, and she'll have none of it. Ananthi is Ellilan's wife, the face and voice of many who have all but given up hope of ever finding the 'disappeared'.

The Tamils' complicated love-hate relationship with the LTTE was overlaid with an undercurrent of fear and resentment that ripples through every interaction with outsiders, be it Sinhala or Indian. Lankan Tamils half relished that they finally had a fighting force to stand up to the Sinhala majority, but it was a Faustian bargain. Honour and self-pride in return for blood, guts and sacrifice.

~

Free Jaffna

In 1998, as part of a group of international journalists invited by the Sri Lankan government to take a tour of 'free Jaffna', I got a taste of what it was like to live under the Sri Lankan jackboot and, at the same time, the watchful eye of the Tigers. One had to take flights operated by the SLAF, from the Ratmalana airbase in Colombo, sitting cheek by jowl with Sri Lankan military personnel who were flying out to relieve those stationed in and around the Palaly airbase.

The runway was a reminder of the most recent battle for Jaffna; it was so pitted and cratered that we skittered across on landing and take-off. An airbase and a city 16 kilometres apart, conjoined by an uneasy peace. Sri Lankan forces had evicted every single villager from homes and farms within a 16-kilometre radius of Palaly. The dirt road was flanked by home after empty home, abandoned cattle sheds, school buildings with their roofs and walls blown off, tiny tea shops, toddy outlets that must have once done thriving business. It was no man's land—barren fields lay untended, overgrown, ringed with palmyra trees and the dense, lush greenery of a countryside that must have once sustained a bustling community; the once well-off residents herded into what were little more than slums in the heart of Jaffna.

I got a stark sense of what it must have felt like to be in the cross hairs of the LTTE and the IPKF when the bus taking us to Jaffna city dropped us right in front of the Jaffna Teaching Hospital. The building still bore the scars of the so-called 'Diwali day shootout' by the Indian Army on doctors, patients and staff, all in uniform, on 21 October 1987. An attack which the Indian Army justified claiming it was retaliatory fire. The LTTE, it would later emerge, had allegedly sent some of its wounded to be treated here.

Some eleven years later, the hospital was teeming with patients, mostly women and children. The few men were either old or wounded, many with prosthetic limbs, but with an erudition that came through even during the briefest of interactions.

Wealthy Tamils from an era that predated an LTTE-dominated Jaffna had always prided themselves on the education provided by the missionaries who had set up schools and colleges across the country some 250 years ago. That led to a whole generation of prominent Lankan Tamils being educated here before going abroad to the UK and the US for higher studies.

The Jaffna they left behind remained inextricably tied with the many Tamil movements, the alphabet soup of parties, that came up to challenge Colombo's dominance. Ultimately, of course, the LTTE emerged as the pre-eminent voice for Tamil nationalism after the Prabhakaran-led group decimated and brutally silenced Tamil moderates, justifying extreme violence as the means to an end.

As an old Lanka hand told me, 'In India, if you disagree, they vote you out. In Lanka, they just kill you . . .'

In this highly politicized city where everyone is an expert, the bloodletting ever since the majoritarian versus minority politics took hold turned even mild-mannered academics into gun-toting Tamil separatists.

As anyone with links to the violent separatists was targeted, taken away at random for questioning or simply eliminated, alienated Tamils sympathetic to the cause were drawn to those who posed as their saviours. The LTTE's commitment to and fierce avowal of the Tamil cause—more than the other separatist groups who were accused of striking side-deals with Colombo and Delhi—ensured the Prabhakaran-led 'nationalists' would rise in prominence to become the bulwark of the resistance. In drawing on an empathetic populace that would become their eyes and ears, and heed their diktat, a vast intelligence-gathering network was created, which would undermine every outside force that attempted to subjugate it.

Yet, one could never be sure if the Jaffna Tamil—then as much as now—was an enthusiastic supporter who wholeheartedly backed the violent means adopted by the LTTE in their quest for Eelam, or if he simply played along, looking all the while over his shoulder, worried that he and his family would not be able to dodge the LTTE bullet unless he did what was asked of him.

Was the violence, the heartbreak of losing loved ones and their broken homes worth it, one had wondered then—as one does now—because the community had come to realize that the quid pro quo of such a force multiplier was that a whole generation of the young had no real future except to take up arms. Clearly, this was why families who could afford to smuggle their children out, did so at great cost, but the poorer sections had little choice but to stay and face conscription.

This was brought home as I wandered around that morning and processed the misery that hung like a pall of gloom over the hospital. Until then I had only heard of child soldiers which, many said, was mere government propaganda. As I was the only Tamil-speaking journalist in that group, the women in the Jaffna Teaching Hospital opened up to me that day. None would share her name, but every one of them spoke of how they had quietly moved their children out, as any child, boy or girl, between the ages of thirteen and eighteen was fair game for LTTE recruiters. If the LTTE found out, retaliation would be swift and brutal, they said. If the boy had been sent abroad, the girl would be forced to take his place.

One woman said to me, lowering her voice, 'Can you see a single child, a single teenager on the street?' I looked around, and realized she was right. 'There's no man above eighteen and no man below thirty here, and no girls, no young women. Nobody's safe. We are a city of old people,' she said.

'The Pulikal (Tigers) want to save us—that's why they have left Jaffna. But they haven't really left, so we are watched by everyone—the government and the Tigers,' said another woman, urging me to leave, worried they would attract attention.

The Bishop of Jaffna, sheltering hundreds of families in the sprawling bishopric was equally cagey. When asked if the return to Jaffna was an indication that the people had grown weary of the LTTE and were voting with their feet, the bishop had me quickly ushered out of the premises rather than be pinned down on where he stood vis-à-vis the Tigers.

The hold that the LTTE had over the people, a mix of admiration and fear, was best illustrated when the grim-faced owner of a hotel where I stayed on a subsequent visit to Jaffna trotted out the LTTE line that under the Tigers, women were completely safe, even as he quietly asked me to lock my door that night!

In Kilinochchi, ahead of an interview with S.P. Thamilchelvam, the LTTE political ideologue, a decade later, I noted that the mindset hadn't changed. My LTTE minder tried to lock me into my room at St Theresa's Convent, a stone's throw from the LTTE headquarters. I persuaded him to give the key back, saying I was claustrophobic, and promised him I wouldn't venture out. Later that night, I broke that promise as I woke to a rumble on the dark main street in an otherwise deathly quiet town, and stepped out to see tanks and trucks towing two fighter planes. It was only when the newly formed Air Tigers bombed Colombo in April 2009 that I realized what he was trying to prevent me from seeing.

My LTTE minder was the media in-charge Dhaya Master, who would be brought in by the Sri Lanka Army to identify Prabhakaran's bullet-riddled body when he was found in Nanthikadal in May 2009. In 2015, he refused to answer any questions on where he and other LTTE remnants stood.

~

A Tamil Torn

The dichotomy that characterized the Tamil psyche when the LTTE chief's writ ran here could be put down to a people biding their time until the Prabhakaran era ended, and with it, the guns and violence and suicide bomb squads. They may have had enough of allowing one force to dictate how they must think, act and feel. Did they ever feel trapped, unable to escape the wrath of a man who claimed to speak for them but never let them speak their mind, all the while dogged by a state that saw them as the fifth column for their embrace of the LTTE's brand of terror?

C.V.K. Sivagnanam, the chairman of the newly elected National Provincial Council, had no qualms at all in standing up strongly for Prabhakaran when I asked if the Tamil people are relieved now that he's gone. 'Without the LTTE, we would have had nobody to fight for the rights of the Tamil people.' This was a full year after landmark elections empowered Tamil politicians who had disavowed their ties to the militant separatists.

Indicating that the opposite sentiment prevailed, he said that the Tamil people owed the LTTE chief a huge debt of gratitude. 'We owe him. Prabhakaran is the only one who was willing to stand up for our rights as equal citizens of this country and when that failed, fight for the cause, fight for Tamil Eelam and not compromise on that stand. That's why Tamils will never criticize him, we could never do that.'

The Rajiv Gandhi legacy—the constitutional route to equality—stood for nought around the dinner table that night in Jaffna as no one disagreed on the violent methods that were embraced by the radicalized Tamil. A virtual who's who of Jaffna's brains trust, politicians and businessmen, they had all at one time or the other interacted with the Tiger supremo as he grew from heading one of many groups that came up to counter Colombo, to helming the only group that mattered. Prabhakaran, the virtual messiah, his rush to megalomania never challenged.

~

Prabhakaran Legatees Rejected by Electorate

Was Sivagnanam's the popular view? Post the Prabhakaran era, a clutch of moderate political parties such as the umbrella Ilankai Thamil Arasu Katchi (ITAK) has risen anew from the ashes of the LTTE, bringing together LTTE remnants and pro–LTTE-leaning politicians, like Gajan Ponnambalam of the Tamil National People's Front (TNPF).

While many older Sri Lankan Tamils who had pandered to the LTTE's militaristic political order continue to hold a candle for Prabhakaran, there are many who believe in a unitary Sri Lanka and want the current process to go forward. These Tamils, outside the charmed circle of Prabhakaran and his hand-picked commanders and their families, survived the war years by staying well below the radar as power shifted back and forth between the Tigers and the army, and as the city changed hands over thirty years in the often futile and bloody tug of war between the secessionists and those who believed in federal freedoms.

Jaffna Tamils with a history of staunch anti-Sinhala activism, like Ponnambalam, for instance, have made a conscious decision to paper over the disquiet that they are back to being second-class citizens after three decades of fighting for self-rule. The weapons Ponnambalam uses today might be different, falling back on the Constitution and the right to dissent rather than Prabhakaran. But in a clear message that times were changing, Ponnambalam's party, the TNPF, was rejected by the electorate in the 2015 elections for attempting to nail its flag to the LTTE.

The TNPF's main electoral plank was a call to reject the Rajapaksa government's division of the north and the east. This was done by the Sri Lankan President when the North-Eastern Province was de-merged in 2007, following a court verdict that rejected Jayewardene's 1988 proclamation of a merger as part of the Rajiv–Jayewardene accord. Rajapakse also watered down the powers given to the newly created Northern Provincial Council, placing the police and the courts under Colombo's jurisdiction, instead of implementing the full-fledged devolution that had been promised under the accord. But in a sign of the times, a political party like Ponnambalam's tagged to Prabhakaran, however well-meaning its intent, found no takers.

Ponnambalam still hankers after the unfulfilled promise of the 13th Amendment. 'We will fight until we get a joint north-east provincial council, not this truncated one where the north and the east have been divided, as well as full devolution. Do you know that even the devolution that was promised by the Indo-Sri Lankan agreement by Rajiv Gandhi does not go far enough? I have always argued against it in that form,' he insists.

In the northern swathe of towns and villages where the needs of the Tamil individual had for so long been subsumed by the Prabhakaran-run Tamil state, the anger, resentment and shock at the comprehensive defeat of their forces and the manner of the implosion, have given way to a grudging acceptance that while fate may have dealt them a low blow, all has not been lost. It was up to them to make the best of it and take another shy at the earlier yen for parliamentary debate and the rule of law.

The biggest change in the once embattled north is the open, thrusting debate on the streets and in homes about Tamil rights and privileges, the animated discussion and vitriol by an elected council of Sri Lankans of Tamil origin where diametrically opposite views are aired—one side unapologetically accusing the current administration led by Chief Minister Wigneswaran of selling out to Colombo, the other stressing the need to work alongside the Sinhala majority to heal the wounds of nearly four decades of war.

~

Sampanthan—The Man in the Middle

This is Jaffna's first real taste of democracy post the internecine wars that began in the 1980s. Can it let the opportunity slip away in the welter of criticism of Colombo that is threatening to drown out even those like the venerable TNA leader and member of Parliament Rajavarothiam Sampanthan who counsels patience and negotiation? The newly anointed éminence grise of Tamil politicians, Sampanthan lays out the reasoning behind the moderate stance of his party.

'This is an opportunity in Sri Lankan history that has not presented itself in over sixty years. There is the very real possibility here of a brand new dawn. We have the chance to work out an amicable arrangement; the voices of the people of the north and the east and all the other Tamils are being given a hearing, and we would be very remiss not to grab the moment, the opportunity, with both hands and work with the government on securing a future for the Tamil people who have suffered for long enough,' he said.

Most significant was the casting out by the Sri Lankan people of the one man who not only crushed the Tigers but also opposed the rehabilitation of the thousands of Tamils dispossessed by the 2009 Eelam War IV—Mahinda Rajapakse.

'The defeat of Mahinda Rajapaksa has opened new possibilities for our country. It has brought in a Parliament and a government that is not majoritarian. There is a shift, a change,' he said. 'The important thing is that we have the broad support of all Tamil parties on framing a new Constitution, with a proposed aim to bring in amendments that will work to benefit the Tamil people.'

Sampanthan himself made history of sorts when he was nominated—by the same Sinhalese majority that had been dubbed chauvinist by the Tamils—as the leader of the Opposition in Parliament, thus becoming the first Tamil in over thirty years to hold the post.

Except, discrimination against the Tamils is deeply entrenched.

A well-known Tamil-origin media baron—he did not want to be named—who exudes upper-crust class, vocalized a well-known discriminatory tool: 'Even though I don't look like a terrorist, and I'm a known face in the capital and in Jaffna, and drive a luxury car, I am flagged down and asked to produce my identity card and the car number is taken down because the identity card clearly identifies me as a Tamil. My Sinhala-speaking colleague never faces the same treatment.'

Suresh Premachandran, the former PLOTE leader, understands that kind of discriminatory language. At his home in a cul de sac in the suburb of Dehiwala, his brother, Sarvesan, who teaches in Colombo and was heading out to catch a bus to Jaffna that night, echoed the almost universal anger felt by Tamils at their continued victimization.

'The war has been over for six years, but we are still stopped and searched on buses and trains,' says Sarvesan. 'There are different identity cards for each ethnic group—there's one for the Sinhalese, one for the Muslims and one for us. And the police don't even look at the other cards, they always look at mine, because it's in Tamil. This must stop. If they want to integrate us into the mainstream, then it's time every Sri Lankan, whatever his or her ethnic origin, is treated as equal. All our ID cards must be the same.'

On the A9 highway, as we headed to Sencholai a day later, my Tamil driver slowed down before an army patrol. 'Now just see, he will try and find some way to extort money. He will say we were speeding or something.' That is exactly what happened, except that before the army patrol asked any more questions of the hapless driver and we were delayed even further, I bought some tuppenny-ha'penny commemoratives of the Eelam war. And we were smilingly waved on. Two hundred Sri Lankan rupees lighter.

Premachandran who, like Ponnambalam, bit the electoral dust, reserves the bulk of his ire for the Sri Lankan government for going back on Rajiv's Indo-Sri Lankan agreement. Harking back to the recurring theme that resonates across the north on its bifurcation from the east, thus ending the eighteen-year run of the United Provincial Council, Premachandran, like most Tamils, sees the division as a means to cut the Tamils down to size. 'We want the north and the east re-united as was done post the agreement signed by Rajiv Gandhi and JR [Jayewardene],' he said, while railing against the powers of the police to search and detain, which he said had not been curbed for twenty-five years.

Premachandran also brought up the newest irritant—the inability of the elected provincial government to govern. 'No power devolves to the council which is an elected body, as power is vested in the governor and not the chief minister. Till today, this provincial council has no budget, but operates on a grant to meet the 90 per cent recurring expenditure. Just one small change is needed in the Rajiv–JR accord to empower the council,' he says.

'There are 80,000 war widows in the north and the east,' avers Premachandran, 'and 12,000 orphans and some 1000 war wounded. The Northern Council should have at least been allowed to provide for orphans and help rehabilitate and treat the wounded. Instead, we have 1,00,000 Sri Lankan soldiers, a peace-time army that is simply unprepared to help the people in the north and the east. What are they doing here?' he asks with barely concealed scorn. 'Farming?'

He isn't far wrong. Soldiers driving threshers and harvesters are common on the road from Kilinochchi to Vavuniya and Puthukkudiyiruppu.

An equally big bugbear are funds from the diaspora that are available for reconstruction but, by law, cannot be touched. 'The chief minister has been promised funding from the diaspora for the welfare of the war wounded, but he cannot accept it unless a legal proviso is made for the use of these funds.'

Colombo has held back from empowering the Northern Council in the fear that once that is done, the north and east will secede, using the Constitution rather than guns to get what they have long fought for, 'and that we will become powerful again, masters of our own destiny', Premachandran scoffs. He says, however, that the clamour for a federal system of government as it exists in India must be heeded.

Like Sampanthan, many old-timers, including the highly perceptive former vice chancellor of Jaffna University Prof. P. Balasundarampillai and a clutch of other intellectuals and politicians whom I meet one evening in Jaffna at the home of an Indian consulate official, are keen to soothe the 'wounds' of the war. Several had fought under the ITAK banner—funded, many say, by the Tamil diaspora—in the landmark election to the Provincial Council last year, and are looking at ways to secure the future of the Tamil people politically.

The Tamils' embrace of the new political upturn raises several questions. Has the million-strong community completely abandoned its yearning for an independent state after the de facto state-within-the-state, courtesy Prabhakaran, which had given them the status of first-class citizens, was snatched away? Or are they still holding on to the hope that the hugely wealthy diaspora in Europe and Canada that had backed their battle once before, will come together again and fund another Tamil army to chip away at the dominant Sinhalese? If not justice, then retribution?

Sampanthan will have none of it, saying the imputation that Tamils would go back to violence and guns is downright laughable.

The man in the vanguard of the anti-Colombo refrain in Jaffna is Northern Provincial Council Chief Minister Wigneswaran. A respected retired judge from Colombo who was hand-picked for the job by Sampanthan, Wigneswaran is equally certain there will be no turning back the clock. But his campaign to rehabilitate war widows and the war wounded, and bring in investment for capacity-building and reconstruction by wooing India has run aground. Almost apoplectic with anger and frustration, Wigneswaran is constrained by the constitutional requirement that has overridden the 13th Amendment—that a governor, who is entrusted with more powers and answers only to Colombo, has to sign off on every proposal. So far, the governor hasn't.

More lawyer-politician than economist, Wigneswaran, a Colombo native, knows he must guard against his fellow Tamils going back to believing that the gun is the only answer to their ills. He must keep their faith in the federal model alive and, at the same time, not be seen as Colombo's cat's paw, all too willing to do the Sirisena government's bidding.

His one-point agenda that overrides all else is to restore to the Tamil people their sense of self-respect, and the first step towards that is to get every single soldier from the Sri Lanka Army off the city streets, even though the army itself believes its presence is necessary to ensure the continuing security of the north and the east. Tamils make up a population of roughly 1.6 million here, where the military has deployed 1,50,000–2,00,000 troops.

Again, as he freely admits, 'I have had no success with that either.'

As the army razes mile after mile of graveyards and tombstones that once, albeit ghoulishly, commemorated the Tamil Tigers martyred to the cause, erasing the last reminders of thirty years of the miseries of war, the Tamils of Sri Lanka know that the path to redemption cannot lie with yet another Prabhakaran.

Epilogue

THE PALALY OF OCTOBER 2015 is a world away from the one that I had seen on my previous visits. A barometer of the change that has overtaken the north is the runway and, in fact, the entire airbase—picture-perfect, rebuilt by the Manmohan Singh government as a gesture of goodwill.

The threat of war has long receded. No longer does it look as if it is bracing for an attack, for sudden conflict.

The only sign that it is still an active airbase comes from the SLAF aircraft that has landed just ahead of us. That, and the lone artillery gun at the far end of the runway, jutting out through sandbags against a cloudless blue sky. A helicopter hovers noisily overhead, while around us, fresh young recruits—men and women—are being put through their paces early in the morning.

Six years after the war ended, the SLAF has gone commercial with a vengeance. The last seat on a round trip via Trincomalee's scenic China Bay on the newly renamed Heli Tours aircraft doesn't come cheap. Ratmalana airbase in Colombo is awash with stewardesses and staff in smart new uniforms manning check-in counters that have replaced the rickety desks of the past. And the fifty-seater that takes off for the Palaly airbase is filled not just with servicemen and their young families, but dozens of well-heeled members of the Tamil diaspora, many returning to Jaffna for the first time since the war ended, along with insurance salesmen and businessmen.

Devi, a chic London-based former resident of Sri Lanka stands out with her fashionably short crop of grey and her designer handbag. Accompanied by her daughters, a grand-daughter, a British son-in-law and her husband, she is going to check on her grandmother's home in Kankesanthurai—a house she has inherited but hasn't seen since she left the country over thirty years ago.

'My daughters were barely three and five when we last came here,' she says. Emotional, not sure what she will find, she shows me pictures of a home that had borne the brunt of the war, first taken over by the IPKF and then the Sri Lanka Navy. Its roof had been blown off, some of the walls had caved in, and around it was nothing but desolation. She is keen to rebuild her turn-of-the-century home. Her husband, who came from Chavakachcheri, further east, which bore the brunt of all four Eelam wars, isn't sure what they should do.

On the way back to Colombo a few days later, we meet again at the Heli Tours office in Jaffna city.

Their mood is markedly different. Any hopes they had of rebuilding have been tempered by the reality of maintaining a house so far from what they had called home for nearly forty years. 'I would much rather sell it,' the husband says to me, out of his family's earshot, as they head back to Colombo and on to the tranquillity of Galle for a destination holiday by the sea.

Six years since the *prachanai*—the troubles—came crashing down around their ears, the rage among the Tamils is waning. But the new government, an amalgam of two parties, the SLFP and the UNP, both ideologically opposed and arch-rivals, but united against Mahinda Rajapaksa, would do well not to take the Tamil community for granted.

The fury that once consumed the Tamils in the north and the east, fanned for thirty long years by Prabhakaran, with his masterly ability to inspire fear and adulation in equal measure, is no doubt greatly diminished. Where once there was seething anger bubbling just below the surface, drawing satisfaction from acts of revenge against the Sinhalese army of occupation, with no apologies proffered for the violence and brutality visited on the Lankan soldiery or Rajiv Gandhi's assassination, today, there isn't regret, but instead a pang for a lost cause, an entire missing generation. And overlaying it all, fatigue.

There's a weary acknowledgment that the Tigers who spoke out for them and fought in their name, had been outflanked and out-manoeuvred not just by Colombo, but by the Tamils' greatest and most vocal supporters—the EU and Oslo. And with them, by a Washington and Delhi that could ill afford another cataclysmic 9/11, an IPKF disaster, or a Mumbai of 26/11. No outside power would countenance the separatist cause.

The language of war, of bluster and braggadocio is at an end. The Tamils in Jaffna are speaking a whole new vernacular. They know they have drawn the short end of the stick, that they must swallow their pride when asked by Sinhala-speaking policemen—and the numerous army patrols—deployed across the cities of the north, from Jaffna to Vavuniya and Kilinochchi, to show their ID cards. They are the vanquished, not the victors.

~

The hopes and aspirations of the people of Jaffna no longer lie with Kilinochchi but with Colombo and, once again, with New Delhi. India has responded by reaching out to the ordinary Tamil, building 50,000 homes to rehabilitate the displaced and the homeless, and rebuilding schools and hospitals, while diplomatically using every lever to ensure that the minority community is no longer neglected or treated like second-class citizens.

The Indian mission's largesse has, however, left the 75,000 Tamil-speaking Muslims out of the reckoning, warns academic Ahilan Kadirgamar. He is a distant relative of the slain foreign minister Lakshman Kadirgamar, and one of the many intellectuals who have returned to Jaffna to highlight the issues that confront a post-war north, including the plight of war widows turning to prostitution and the fate of the 'disappeared'.

For the young, Europe and Canada still beckon. Foreign language institutes dot the Jaffna landscape, offering French, German and English courses. 'When someone is learning English, you know he wants to go to a university abroad for higher studies, and if it's German it's probably because he wants to get a technical degree. If it's French, then she's probably looking for a husband . . .' says an irreverent Tamil returnee.

For all the dark humour, Jaffna exemplifies the challenge before all Tamils—they know that this time they have to drive the hardest of bargains, while eschewing violence and strictly playing by the rules. This time, as they rebuild their shattered lives and homes, they must put a new leadership in place and hope that their collective voice of reason will water down the jingoism of the Sinhala majority that continues to shrug away the slights to tetchy Tamil pride.

Despite the sense of a new beginning and the perception that Jaffna stands on the cusp of a transformation, Prof. Pillai says—echoing what many old-timers feel—that with his children working in the UK and unlikely to return, even as question marks remain over the newly elected government and the provincial council's ability to deliver justice to war-affected families, he didn't see much point in holding on to his ancestral home.

Questions on where the ordinary Tamil stands as far as his politics, faith and societal standing are concerned, remain. For the Sri Lankan Tamil there are existential dilemmas that need to be resolved. The war had ended, Prof. Pillai said, but the grievances of Tamils defeated in the war, were yet to be addressed. 'My wife and I aren't sure as yet, but when I retire, maybe I'll sell my home and go and live with my son and daughter.'

That's probably why at the Palaly airbase, where even today nobody enters or leaves without an SLAF escort, neither the glorious sunshine, the abundance of cheerful bougainvillea that line the runway nor the happy tourists deplaning can chase away the ghosts of the past.

In this city of the defeated, of battles lost that could never have been won, at least, not in perpetuity, Jaffna, which epitomizes the heart and soul of the Ilankai Thamil, seems to have all but shaken off thirty years of ennui, of the endless wait for the night to end, for the tide to turn.

It is no longer a city in retreat, not defeatist by any stretch of the imagination. Instead, it seems like the Lankan Tamils are finally done waiting for someone, be it a Rajiv Gandhi or a Prabhakaran, a white knight or the prince of darkness, to come to their rescue, and have taken matters into their own hands. This is their battle to fight, their war to win—but without guns and violence.

Despite all the naysayers and the doomsday projections by a clutch of writers and commentators, the Sri Lankan Tamil has gone from bust to boom. It's still work in progress. But there's no one and nothing to hold them back but themselves.

~

Across the narrow seas, in the serene, green expanse of Sriperumbudur, stands a memorial to Rajiv Gandhi to mark the spot where he had been assassinated. The high points of his tenure are many—he was elected with one of the biggest majorities in Indian history, he forged peace with the Sikhs without alienating the moderates, extended a hand of friendship to the Mizos, reached out to Beijing and Islamabad, took the first steps towards empowering the poorest of the poor in Indian villages by introducing panchayati raj and became the first to see the potential of India's booming middle class as a boost for the economy—but his Sri Lankan misadventure may yet overshadow it all. Unless the Sri Lankan Tamil reclaims the lost legacy of Rajiv Gandhi, the man who offered them a promised land which his nemesis, Prabhakaran—consumed by violence, speaking only of vengeance and retribution—could never deliver.

Index